BERLITZ®

PARIS

1987/1988 Edition

By the staff of Berlitz Guides
A Macmillan Company

How to use our guide

- All the practical information, hints and tips that you will need before and during the trip start on page 100.

- For general background, see the sections Paris and the Parisians, p. 6, and A Brief History, p. 12.

- All the sights to see are listed between pages 22 and 76. Our own choice of sights most highly recommended is pinpointed by the Berlitz traveller symbol.

- Entertainment, nightlife and all other leisure activities are described between pages 76 and 91, while information on restaurants and cuisine is to be found on pages 93 to 99.

- Finally, there is an index at the back of the book, pp. 125–127.

Found an error or an omission in this Berlitz Guide? Or a change or new feature we should know about? Our editor would be happy to hear from you, and a postcard would do. Be sure to include your name and address, since in appreciation for a useful suggestion, we'd like to send you a free travel guide.

Although we make every effort to ensure the accuracy of all the information in this book, changes occur incessantly. We cannot therefore take responsibility for facts, prices, addresses and circumstances in general that are constantly subject to alteration.

Text: Jack Altman
Photography: cover, pp. 4–5, 6, 7, 13, 21, 34, 39, 45, 62, 69, 71, 72, 85 Monique Jacot; pp. 9, 15, 22, 31, 33, 53, 59, 60, 75, 81, 82, 87, 88, 89, 91 Loomis Dean; pp. 10, 36, 43, 47, 49, 54, 57, 65, 66, 79, 92, 97 Erling Mandelmann; p. 19 A. Held; pp. 28, 77 PRISMA
We wish to thank Suzanne Patterson and Claire Teeuwissen for their help with this guide, and we're also grateful to the Office de Tourisme de Paris and the Office national français du Tourisme for their valuable assistance.
Cartography: Falk-Verlag, Hamburg

Contents

Paris and the Parisians

The city and the people of Paris share a boundless self-confidence that exudes from every stone in its monuments and museums, bistrots and and boutiques, from every chestnut tree along its avenues and boulevards, from every little street-urchin, fashion model, butcher and baker, from every irate motorist and every charming maître d'hôtel. It is a self-confidence that will exhilarate anyone open to the breathless adventure of Paris, though it may intimidate people who dislike the light, movement and noise of life itself.

Some see it spilling over into arrogance—in the bombast of monumental architecture or in the overbearing attitudes of know-it-all street-philosophers. But looking around, you must admit they have something to be arrogant about. Stand on the

Pont Royal in the late afternoon and gaze down the Seine to the glass-panelled Grand Palais, bathed in the pink-and-blue glow of the river's never tranquil waters. Already you sense that the light in this City of Light is of a very special kind, bringing phosphorescence to the most commonplace little square or side-street. In case the message is not clear, Paris offers unparalleled night-time illumination of its major historic buildings, avenues and squares, underscored by the ongoing battle between the city's monument-cleaners and automobile pollution.

Despite inevitable erosions of social change, Paris manages to sustain most of its myths and legends. Take the jargon of its topography, for example,

Something old, something new, something borrowed—and something blue.

names that evoke not just a place but a state of mind.

The Right Bank conjures up an image of bourgeois respectability. Historically the stronghold of merchants and royalty, it remains today the home of commerce and government. Faubourg Saint-Honoré offers the luxury of *haute couture* and jewellery shops and the authority of the president's palace (and the British embassy), while the Champs-Elysées claims the first-run cinemas, airline companies and car showrooms.

The Left Bank, on the other hand, has always had a bohemian and intellectual image, dating back to the founding of the university and the monasteries. Today the Sorbonne, the Académie française, the publishing houses and myriad bookshops continue to exert an intellectual magnetism. Left Bank theatres typically prefer avant-garde drama to the boulevard comedy of the Right Bank.

The art galleries, doubtless needing the sustenance both of business and the intelligentsia, are about equally divided between Right and Left Banks, though the establishment-oriented galleries seem to be more in evidence on the Right Bank. The artists themselves remain characteristically on the periphery of both Right and Left Banks, in Montmartre and Montparnasse respectively.

A constant flow and interchange of citizenry from one bank to the other takes place over the bridges of the Seine, a very accessible river well integrated into the town's life.

Paris is a city of people constantly on the move, at all hours of day and night—inevitable, really, since it's one of the most densely populated urban centres in the world. In nearly every one of Paris's 20 *arrondissements,* or districts, you will find shops, offices and apartments side by side and on top of each other, which makes the city's streets exceedingly lively. Don't be surprised if you become addicted to Paris's most marvellous sport—watching the world from a café table.

From that vantage point you can easily check on another of the town's legends—that of the good-looking women. The emphasis is not so much on "beautiful" or "pretty" but quite simply "good-looking". You may note that Parisian women are by and large *not* more or less pretty than elsewhere,

Hunting for bargains—whether in fashions, antiques, prints or stamps —is an absorbing Paris pastime.

but somehow they manage, with a colour combination, a hairstyle, a scarf tied in a particular way, but above all in the way they sit, stand or walk, to just *look* good. Drawing on that communal self-confidence, they convince themselves—and nearly everybody else.

The key to the joy of just sitting and watching Paris go by is in the endless variety of the people. There is no "Parisian" type, physically speaking. The town's 2 million population is drawn from every region in France—Brittany, Alsace, Burgundy, Provence, for example —and the Parisian's traditional contempt for the "provinces"

is matched only by his fierce regional loyalty to the distant home of his ancestors, most often just one generation removed.

However dominant Paris may be in French art, literature, music, fashion, education, scientific research, commerce and politics, one area has been denied it—cuisine. There is no such thing as Parisian cuisine. This has the advantage, if you are a first-time visitor to France, of letting you come to the capital and sample each of the country's regional cuisines as you pick your way among the 11,000 or more bistrots and restaurants around town. Often a region's representative restaurants cluster around the railway station serving that area—like the Breton restaurants around the Gare Montparnasse—for that is where yesterday's "provincials" stopped off and set up home as Parisians.

These "provincials" were drawn, like people the world over, to a city conceived and evolved on the grand scale but offering at the same time an intimacy on the neighbourhood level. While avenues and boulevards sweep up to

Pigalle, with famed Moulin Rouge, lives on in round-the-clock whirl.

monumental vistas, the narrow streets around the church of Saint-Séverin lead back to medieval times and the Rue de Varenne to the gracious classicism of the 18th century. In the same way, the Parisian has an imposing, sometimes forbidding reputation, but also wit, style and charm in his personal dealings that make him much more accessible than you would expect.

Paris has the astounding treasures of the Louvre and the ambitious Beaubourg cultural centre. But it also offers those tiny storefronts on the Rue Jacob for collections of old artistic playing cards and Napoleonic tin soldiers. You can spend a small fortune on the most fabulous evening dress or buy the most stylish tee-shirt—for a thousand times less.

Don't expect to find any amazing bargains in the City of Light. Paris has been around long enough to learn the correct price for everything. The nightlife of the cabarets, theatres, opera, discotheques and nightclubs is *not* cheap, but it *is* still gay, and it is still an adventure. The real bargain is the magic of that light, movement and noise around the Paris streets. That costs just a little shoe leather. **11**

A Brief History

It all began in the middle of the river. Some Celtic fishermen and boatmen called Parisii set up their homes on an island in the Seine—the Ile de la Cité of today. The swiftly flowing waters provided good protection against invaders until the Romans conquered the town in 52 B.C. It was known as Lutetia or Lutèce, meaning marshland.

In Roman times the right bank of the river was too marshy to live on—so the town expanded to the Left Bank. Excavations have revealed the Roman arena, popular for the usual fights between gladiators, lions and Christians, and the public baths (see p. 73), dating from the 2nd and 3rd centuries A.D.

St. Denis brought Christianity to the city and was rewarded by decapitation on the hill of Montmartre. Legend and popular depictions of the event have Denis picking up his head and walking away with it.

Towards the end of the 3rd century Lutetia was overrun by barbarians, mostly Huns and Franks, and the town's inhabitants moved back to the fortified Ile de la Cité. Attila headed this way in 451 but the fervour of St. Geneviève's prayers is said to have persuaded him to spare the city. Clovis, King of the Franks, who showed good faith by converting to Christianity, arrived in 508 and settled down in the Palais de la Cité (now Palais de Justice). People moved back to the Left Bank and the church of Saint-Germain-des-Prés was built in the 6th century.

The Middle Ages

But Paris remained a backwater of the European scene until Hugues Capet established himself there in 987 and made Paris the economic and political capital of France for the Capetian dynasty. Under Louis VI (1108–37) Paris enjoyed its "agricultural age", when enclosed farms, *clos*, flourished. But the strength of Paris was its merchants who exploited the commerce of the Seine by collecting duties and taxes from ships passing through Paris, making the town rich under the motto: *Fluctuat nec mergitur* (It floats but it doesn't sink).

These revenues enabled Philippe Auguste (1180–1223) to construct Notre-Dame cathedral, a fortress named the Louvre, aqueducts, fresh-water fountains and some paved streets. To protect his investment while away on the Third Crusade, he surrounded the growing city with walls.

Leering gargoyles roost on Notre-Dame, keeping Evil at bay.

Louis IX (1226–70) developed the spiritual and intellectual side of Paris life by building the Gothic masterpiece, the Sainte-Chapelle, and many colleges on the Left Bank, including that of Robert de Sorbon (see p. 54). With a population of 100,000, Paris was the largest city in Western Christendom.

The mercantile backbone of the city proved itself in the 14th century when plague and the Hundred Years' War devastated France, leaving Paris at the mercy of the English. In 1356, with King Jean le Bon taken prisoner at Poitiers, the provost of the city merchants, Etienne Marcel, profited from the confusion and set up a municipal dictatorship. Though assassinated a year later, Marcel had showed that the Parisians themselves were a force to be 13 reckoned with in France's history. The next king, Charles V, ever wary of Parisian militancy, built the Bastille fortress.

If the strife of the 14th century had been unsettling for Paris, that of the 15th was positively disastrous. In 1407, the Duke of Burgundy had the Duke of Orleans murdered on Rue Barbette, which led to 12 years of strife between the Burgundians and Armagnacs. The carnage ended only with the capture of Paris by the English in 1420. Ten years later Joan of Arc tried and failed to liberate the town. The next year came the ultimate humiliation with the crowning of the young English King Henry VI at Notre-Dame as King of France. In case that was not enough, the plague of 1466 felled thousands of Parisians.

Paris Takes Shape

Nonetheless the city remained resilient. With François Ier (1515–47), Paris learned to thrive under an absolutist and absentee monarch, busy with wars in Italy and even a year's imprisonment in Spain. The arts, sciences and literature flourished. Much of the Louvre was torn down and rebuilt along its present lines. A new Hôtel de Ville (town hall) was begun, as well as the superb

Saint-Eustache church. The Parisians were already assuming that distinctive pride over the uniqueness of their town. Poet Pierre de Ronsard saw Paris as "the city imbued with the discipline and glory of the Muses".

The religious wars wreaked havoc and mayhem in Paris, starting in 1572 with the Massacre of St. Bartholomew—3,000 Protestants were killed—and culminating in the siege of the city by Henri de Navarre

in 1589. Before the Catholic League capitulated, 13,000 Parisians had died of starvation. Henri was crowned at Chartres and finally entered the city in 1594—but not before he had turned Catholic. His famous words, "Paris is well worth a mass", have remained an ambiguous comment on the merely political value attached to religion and the special desirability of the French capital. Paris's myth was growing.

Henri IV did Paris proud once he was its master. He built the beautiful Place des Vosges and Place Dauphine, embellished the river banks with the Quais de l'Arsenal, de l'Horloge and des Orfèvres and constructed the Samaritaine hydraulic machine that pumped

The Conciergerie was the last stop for many on their way to the guillotine.

fresh water to Right Bank households till 1813. By far the most popular of France's monarchs, Henri IV was a notorious ladies' man and was known to his subjects as the Vert Galant. He completed the Pont-Neuf (despite its name, the city's oldest standing bridge) and the adjacent gardens, where he had been known to dally with his ladies. Young lovers carry on the tradition there today.

Under Louis XIII (1610–43), Paris began to take on the "fashionable" aspect that has become its mark. The Cours-la-Reine, precursor of the Champs-Elysées, was built for Henri's widow Marie de Médicis. Elegant houses went up along the Faubourg Saint-Honoré, and tree-lined boulevards stretched clear across the city over to the Bastille, creating the airy sweep of modern Paris. The capital also consolidated its position as the hub of the country—with the establishment of the royal printing press, Cardinal Richelieu's Académie française and other scientific institutions such as the botanical gardens, and Paris's new ecclesiastical status as an archbishopric. The cardinal also deserves credit for the splendid Palais-Royal. With the Ile Saint-Louis—formed from two separate islands in 1614 by engineer Christophe Marie—and the residential development of the Marais and Saint-Germain-des-Prés districts, Paris was becoming an increasingly attractive place for nobles from the provinces.

Too much so for the liking of Louis XIV (1643–1715). To bring his overly powerful and independent aristocrats back into line he decided to move the court to Versailles, where palace life was ruinously expensive.

Paris continued to flourish with the landscaping (by Louis' counsellor Jean-Baptiste Colbert) of the Tuileries Gardens, the Champs-Elysées, the construction of the Louvre's great colonnade, the triumphal arches of Saint-Antoine, Saint-Denis and Saint-Martin and the Invalides hospital for soldiers wounded in Louis' wars. The Sun King's fears about Parisian talent for trouble-making led to the innovation of street-lighting (on moonless nights only). The city now numbered 560,000 inhabitants, almost six times as many as in the 13th century under Louis IX.

Paris asserted its cultural ascendancy in Europe with the organization of the academies of the arts, literature and sciences and the founding of the Comédie-Française (1680) and other theatres under Louis XV. Cafés sprang up around the Palais-Royal, and the boulevard life was the animated focus of European intellectual ferment as the Revolution approached.

One of the last constructions of the Ancien Régime, begun in 1784, was a new wall around the city. This became a major factor in the revolutionary unrest, for it was there that the *fermiers-généraux* (financiers) collected taxes from merchants and artisans coming to do business in Paris.

Revolution and Empire

The Revolution of 1789 was more notable for its destruction than for additions to Parisian landmarks—though the removal of the Bastille and the monasteries and convents did create more open spaces. The Revolutionaries made special use of the stronghold of the Capetian dynasty: the Conciergerie in the Palais de Justice, the heart of the medieval kings' palace, became a prison for those condemned by Revolutionary tribunals. And Dr Joseph Guillotin, a member of parliament, who said the times demanded something more humane than the Ancien Régime's hanging, drawing and quartering, developed a new gadget to chop heads off.

With the advent of Napoleon, the city's development resumed. The emperor's frequent absences on foreign business did not hinder his projects for making Paris the capital of Europe. Detailed maps of the city and architectural plans for new buildings were always part of his baggage. Typically he found time during his stop-over in Moscow to work on the reorganization of the Comédie-Française back home. While most visitors see Napoleon's mark in spectacular monuments—the Arc de Triomphe, the 12 avenues of the Etoile, the column of the Grande Armée on Place Vendôme—the emperor himself regarded his most important achievements as those more appropriate to a mayor than a world conqueror: increased supplies of fresh water for the city, the new food-markets, the five slaughter houses and the wine-market. His streamlined municipal administration and police force became a model for modern European urban government.

The centralization of power in the capital also made Paris a potential threat to the govern- **17** ment—the concentration of aggressively ambitious bourgeois, dissatisfied workers and an intellectual class eager to try out its radical ideas. Typically, the Revolution of 1830 came from an alliance of liberal bourgeois Parisian intellectuals, denied the right to publish their newspapers, and the printing-workers thrown into unemployment by the closing of the papers. The 1848 Revolution which ended Louis-Philippe's "bourgeois" monarchy also originated in Paris when the government tried to forbid banquets held in the capital in support of electoral and parliamentary reform. Building Paris up as a great, lively, volatile capital of cultural, social and political innovation automatically turned it into a hotbed of trouble for its rulers.

Modernizing the City

Napoleon III, the great one's nephew, was literally scared into modernizing Paris. He had seen the popular uprisings of 1830 and 1848 flare up in the capital's densely populated working-class neighbourhoods around the city centre and wanted to prevent a recurrence. He commissioned Baron Georges Haussmann to do away with the clusters of narrow streets and alleyways that nurtured discontent and barricades. The baron razed them and moved the occupants out to the suburbs, creating the "red belt" which makes Paris one of the few Western capitals whose suburbia is not predominantly conservative.

The city was opened up by wide boulevards and avenues, giving Paris its modern airy look and highlighting the city's monumental churches and other public buildings. Furthermore, as the baron explained to his emperor, these avenues gave the artillery a clear line of fire in case of revolt.

But this Second Empire was also a time of gaiety and boisterous expansion, emphasized by world fairs in 1855 and 1867, attracting royalty from England, Austria, Russia and Prussia to look at the sparkling new city of Offenbach's operettas and the comedies of Labiche. This was the beginning of "gay Paree".

Then came war, the Franco-Prussian War, with a crippling siege of Paris in 1870 and another uprising, barricades and all. The Paris Commune —self-government of the workers—lasted 10 weeks (March 18

La Belle Epoque—when you could hear Bruant sing at the Chat Noir.

to May 29, 1871), until Adolphe Thiers, first president of the Third Republic, sent in troops from Versailles to crush the revolt.

Into the 20th Century

The Third Republic brought unparalleled prosperity to Paris. Projects begun under Napoleon III, such as the new opera house and the gigantic Halles market (today moved out to the suburbs) were completed in the construction boom that followed the capital's triumphant resurrection after its defeat by the Prussians. By the 1890s Paris had risen to the fore as a cultural magnet. Artists, writers and revolutionaries flocked to this hub of creative activity. Picasso arrived from Barcelona in 1900, followed by Modigliani from Livorno, Soutine from Minsk, Stravinsky from St. Petersburg, Gertrude Stein from San Francisco, and then the long stream of American writers and artists led by Ernest Hemingway and F. Scott Fitzgerald. Paris was Mecca, the myth so powerful that detractors of the Belle Epoque and the Gay Twenties were drowned out by the true believers raising another glass at La Coupole *brasserie* and dancing another foxtrot at Maxim's.

Two wars, of course, took their toll. Though the Germans did not make it to Paris during the First World War, they occupied the city for four drab years (June 1940 to August 1944) in the Second. It took Paris some time to recover. Typically, what the French remember best was the august parade of General de Gaulle and his fellow Resistance fighters down the Champs-Elysées; the expatriates' fondest memory, on the other hand, is of Ernest Hemingway "liberating" the bar of the Ritz Hotel. While much of the cultural magnetism had moved from Paris to New York, the French capital retained some of its mythic character with Jean-Paul Sartre holding existentialist court on the Left Bank and Juliette Greco singing all in black in the jazz-cellars of Saint-Germain-des-Prés.

Students recaptured some of the capital's old revolutionary spirit in May 1968 by hurling the Latin Quarter's paving stones against the smugly entrenched Establishment of de Gaulle's Fifth Republic. President Georges Pompidou affirmed the new prosperity with riverside expressways and skyscrapers, but his crowning achievement was the once controversial, now hugely successful, Beaubourg Cultural Centre.

In 1977, Jacques Chirac became the first democratically elected mayor of Paris. (For over a century, since the turbulent days of the Commune, the national government controlled the city with its own appointed officials.) Now, in a country where politicians can double as mayor and prime minister, Parisians benefit from a leader eager to further national political ambitions with a dynamic municipal performance: cleaner streets, more sports stadiums, tennis courts and swimming pools. Meanwhile, President François Mitterrand has made his own mark with a grand programme, among others, to reorganize the Louvre around a monumental glass pyramid. Paris emerges the winner from these eternal political rivalries.

Left, right or centre, French politicians are a knockout.

What to See

The Seine

The river is by far the best place to begin to take the measure of Paris. Its mixture of grandeur and intimacy is the very essence of the city.

Stand on the Right Bank by the Pont Mirabeau, facing east. Upriver you'll see the Statue of Liberty (a scale-model of the New York original) on the next bridge, framed against the Eiffel Tower over on the Left Bank. This visual melding of the Old and New Worlds prepares you well for the cosmopolitan experience of Paris.

Again and again the Seine provides a spectacular vantage-point for the city's great landmarks. The Eiffel Tower itself, the Palais de Chaillot and Trocadéro Gardens, the Grand and Petit Palais, the Palais-Bourbon, Louvre Museum and Notre-Dame all take on a more enchanting, even dream-like quality if you see them first when floating by in a boat. This is of course even more true of the river's bridges, many of them also monuments to the capital's history.

For that all-important first impression, a **guided boat-trip** on the Seine is unbeatable (see page 27). But this also remains a river to be walked along, despite the encroachments of cars on rapid *voies express* along the banks. You can take delightful strolls right down by the river between the Pont Sully at the eastern end of the Ile Saint-Louis and the Pont de la Concorde and around the two river-islands. Nothing is more restful—and the excitement of Paris demands an occasional rest—than an hour on a bench beneath the poplars and plane trees along the Seine, especially in early morning and late afternoon when that pink Paris light is at its best.

If you want to see the river from its bridges, there are four especially worthy of your attention.

The **Pont-Neuf** (*neuf* means "new") is in fact the oldest stand-

Old prints, magazines and books line stalls on the quais of the Seine. **23**

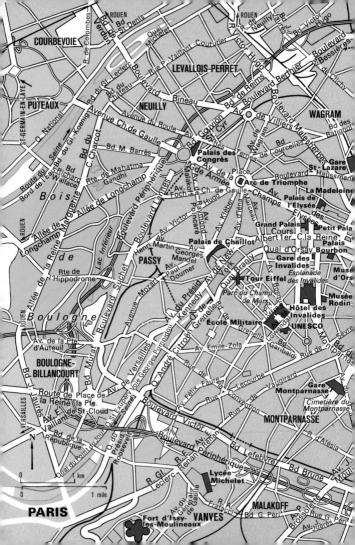

PARIS

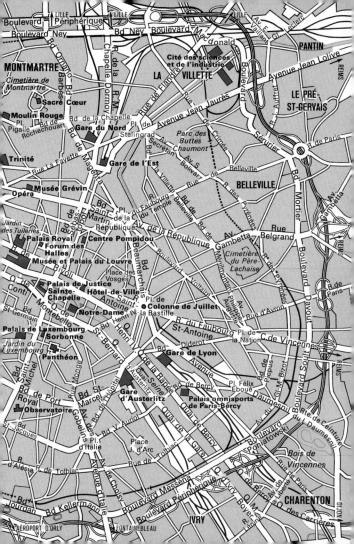

ing bridge in Paris, completed by Henri IV in 1606. It was the first one built without houses: Parisians were pleased to walk across and see their river. It soon became a favourite spot for promenades, for street-singers, charlatans, amateur dentists, professional ladies, pickpockets and above all for the *bouquinistes* selling their old books and pamphlets out of boxes. Established booksellers on the Ile de la Cité were enraged and drove them off to the banks of the Seine, where they have remained ever since.

The **Pont Royal,** built for Louis XIV in 1685, commands a splendid panorama of the Tuileries Gardens and the Louvre. It is the capital's most central bridge in the sense that it offers good views of the Grand and Petit Palais of the *grand-bourgeois* and the Ecole des Beaux-Arts and Institut de France of the intellectual community.

The **Pont de la Concorde,** truly the bridge of the French Revolution, went up between 1787 and 1790. Its support structure used stones from the demolished Bastille prison—especially galling for Royalists in that it was originally Pont Louis XVI. The name was duly changed to Pont de la Révolution the year before Louis was guillotined a couple of hundred yards from the bridge on the Place de la Concorde.

The **Pont Alexandre III,** distinguished architecturally by its single steel arch, represents the final flowering of that bumptiously proud 19th-century industrial spirit exemplified by the Eiffel Tower. The tsar of Russia, Nicholas II, laid the first stone in 1896; the bridge was completed at the turn of the century. The purists find its statues to Fame and Pegasus insufferably bombastic, but lovers view them as an appropriately melodramatic touch to a moonlit stroll beneath the bridge's Belle-Epoque lanterns.

Getting your Bearings

Your orientation in Paris on foot or by car will be simplified by reference to five easily visible landmarks—the Arc de Triomphe and Sacré-Cœur basilica on the Right Bank; the Eiffel Tower and (jarring but nonetheless conveniently visible) Tour Maine-Montparnasse skyscraper on the Left Bank; and Notre-Dame Cathedral in the middle of the Ile de la Cité. Whenever you get lost, you should normally not have to go more than a couple of hundred yards before sighting one of these monuments on the horizon.

Paris by Boat

You can see Paris (and more) from the river and hear multi-lingual commentaries on all the landmarks.

The **Bateaux-Mouches** have open-air or covered seating according to the weather. The standard 75-minute tour starts by the Pont de l'Alma going west to the Pont Mirabeau and turning back upriver to the Pont Sully at the far end of the Ile Saint-Louis. Lunch and dinner cruises (no anoraks or blue jeans, ties obligatory) last 150 minutes (tel. 42.25.22.55).

The **Vedette** or motorboat tours take 60 minutes. Vedettes Paris-Tour Eiffel start at the Pont d'Iéna (Left Bank) and the Quai de Montebello, going west to the Pont de Bir-Hakeim and east to the Pont Sully and back. Vedettes du Pont-Neuf leave from the Pont-Neuf ("illuminated" cruises every evening from May 1 to Oct. 15) to the Eiffel Tower and back (tel. 46.33.98.38).

Leaving from the Quai Anatole France, the **Patache Eautobus** offers half-day cruises to Parc de la Villette north-east of the city via the Seine and the Canal Saint-Martin. Or you could try a one-day cruise up the Seine and the Marne to Nogent (tel. 48.74.75.30).

Right Bank
(Rive Droite)

L'Etoile–Concorde–Palais-Royal

Any tour of the Right Bank should begin at the **Place de l'Etoile** (officially, Place Charles-de-Gaulle), preferably on top of the **Arc de Triomphe.** 🏃 One reason for climbing up Napoleon's gigantic triumphal arch (164 feet high, 148 feet wide) is to get a good view of the 12-pointed star, formed by 12 avenues radiating from the arch in a *tour de force* of geometric planning. The *place,* a vast sloping mound, cannot really be taken in at ground level. The monumental ensemble, conceived by Napoleon as a tribute to France's military glories and heroes, was completed by Baron Haussmann. Over the years the arch has taken on a mythic quality as succeeding régimes have invested it with the spirit of the nation, republican or imperial.

Napoleon himself saw only a life-size wooden and canvas model. Louis-Philippe inaugurated the final version in 1836, complete with bas-reliefs and statuary celebrating victories of the Revolution and Napoleonic empire. It became the tradi- **27**

BRASSERIE
à toute heure

Salade Niçoise ... 28f	Faux filet Béarnaise ... 38f
Salade du Berger ... 28f	Omelet de canard ... 36f
Salade Cubaine ... 28f	Gazpacho ... 22f
Poulet froid garni ... 35f	Quiche Papçouni ... 23f
Assiette des Champs ... 35f	Tarte Provençale ... 23f
Assiette jambon de Paris ... 20f	Croque-monsieur ... 20f
Assiette jambon de pays ... 24f	Croque mixtuité ... 24f
Terrine du Ourcy ... 19f	Omelette nature ... 18f
Rillettes ... 24f	Omelette jambon ... 24f
	Omelette gruyère ... 24f
Spécial lunch ... 21f	Omelette midi ... 28f
Roquefort aux noix ... 24f	Potage de légumes ... 18f
Assiette de gruyère ... 19f	Gratinée ... 24f

HOT·DOG · SANDWICHES
PATISSERIES

tional focus for state funerals of national political, military and even literary heroes—Victor Hugo was given a positively pharaonic tribute here after his death in 1885. In 1920, the Unknown Soldier of World War I was buried at the arch, and three years later the Eternal Flame was lit.

When Hitler came to Paris as a conqueror in 1940, this was the first thing he wanted to see; and, of course, General de Gaulle's triumphant march of Liberation in 1944 started from here.

Avenue Foch, leading away from the Etoile, is the most majestic of the city's residential avenues and the best of the Baron Haussmann's grandiose conceptions. The **Champs-Elysées,** despite extensive commercialization, still deserves the title of the world's most celebrated avenue. It stretches in an absolutely straight line from the Arc de Triomphe to the Place de la Concorde, lined with chestnut trees all the way. The first two-thirds, as you walk down, are devoted to cinemas, shops and café terraces; you'll find the best people-watching

Champs-Elysées or Elysian Fields —abode of the blessed people-watchers.

29

points at the corner of the Avenue George-V on the "shady" side and at Rue du Colisée on the "sunny" side. After the Rond-Point, a pleasant park takes you down to the Place de la Concorde. An interesting theory about the special appeal of the Champs-Elysées is that people look more relaxed and attractive when walking downhill—so ignore the ones going in the other direction.

The **Place de la Concorde** has had a hard time earning its name. More than 1,000 people were guillotined here during the Revolution, the drums rolling to drown out any incendiary words the condemned might utter. In 1934, bloody rioting against the government took place here. Ten years later it was the Germans' last hold in Paris. Today, with floodlit fountains and elegant lamps it is a night-time romance and a daytime adventure, both for the pedestrian pausing to enjoy the vast opening of the Paris sky and for the driver daring to make his way around it. Along with the Etoile, it ranks as one of Europe's greatest challenges to the motorist's ability to survive the centrifugal force that hopefully flings him out to his destination. Smack in the centre you'll see Paris's oldest monument, the 75-foot pink syenite-granite obelisk of Luxor from the temple of Ramses II, dating back to 1300 B.C. For a change it's not something Napoleon brought back from his campaigns but a gift from Mohammed Ali, the viceroy of Egypt, erected in 1836.

After the bustle of the Champs-Elysées and the Place de la Concorde, you'll appreciate the cool, peaceful park, the **Jardin des Tuileries,** named after 13th-century tile works. Its spaciousness is due in large part to the destruction of the Palais des Tuileries during the 1871 Commune (fragments can still be seen by the Jeu de Paume museum in the northwest corner). Children will enjoy the circular ponds on which boats are sailed and sunk almost all year round and the marionette shows in spring and summer.

At the eastern end of the Tuileries stands the **arc de triomphe du Carrousel,** built about the same time as its big brother at the Etoile, visible in a straight line beyond the Luxor Obelisk. This imposing effect

Driving round the Place de la Concorde is one of life's great adventures, especially at rush hour.

was originally planned for Napoleon to see from his bedroom in the Louvre. Today the vista is somewhat spoiled by the skyscrapers of La Défense looming on the horizon.

Leaving the Louvre Museum for a separate visit (see p. 66), cross the Rue de Rivoli to the **Palais-Royal.** There are few pleasanter places to dip back into the history of Paris. Completed in 1639 for the Cardinal Richelieu (after whom it was originally named the Palais-Cardinal), this serene arcaded palace with its garden of limes and beeches and a pond where the young Louis XIV nearly drowned has always been a colourful centre of more or less respectable activity. In the days of Philippe d'Orléans, Regent of France during Louis XV's minority, the Palais-Royal was the scene of notorious orgies. To meet the family's extravagant debts, the ground-floor rooms were turned into boutiques—the last of which still sell old coins, medals, engravings and antiques—and cafés that attracted a fashionable society.

But in Paris the beau monde and demi-monde have always lived off each other, and the Palais-Royal soon took over from the Pont-Neuf as the meeting-place of artists, intellectuals, charlatans, prostitutes and pickpockets. On July 13, 1789, a young firebrand orator, Camille Desmoulins, stood on a table at the Palais-Royal's Café de Foy and made the call to arms that set off the French Revolution the next day. At the other end of that era, Prussian General Blücher came to the Palais-Royal after Waterloo to

J. KLEIN, LAUSANNE

Peaceful area around the Palais-
32 *Royal recalls a more elegant age.*

squander 1,500,000 francs in one night at one of the many rambunctious gambling dens.

East of the Palais-Royal, the old food markets of les Halles (moved to the more hygienic, inevitably less colourful suburb of Rungis) have been replaced by gardens, new apartment buildings and the **Forum des Halles,** a rather garish shopping centre. Around it, the lively neighbourhood of cafés, boutiques and art galleries linking up with the Centre Pompidou (Beaubourg, see p. 68) is very popular with the young crowd. The liveliest meeting-place is around the handsome Renaissance **Fontaine des Innocents** (once part of a cemetery).

On the north side of les Halles, another monument of the Renaissance period, but decidedly Gothic in silhouette, is the church of **Saint-Eustache,** remarkable for its 17th-century stained-glass windows over the choir, crafted according to medieval traditions.

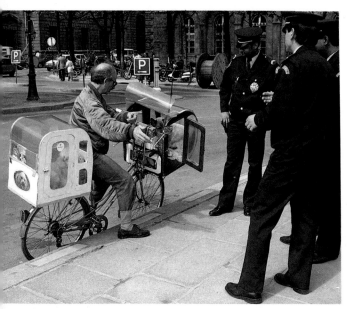

Place Vendôme–Opéra–Madeleine

It's hard to find a more elegant place to work in than the **Place Vendôme,** an airy gracious octagon designed to provide an imposing setting for a statue of Louis XIV. Only his financiers could afford the rents here, and nearly 300 years later the situation has not changed much: there are 19 banks (as well as world-famous jewellers, the Ministry of Justice and the Ritz Hotel) encircling the column with which Napoleon replaced the Sun King. The spiral of bronze bas-reliefs depicting scenes from the Great Battles, topped by a statue of Napoleon himself, was cast from 1,250 cannons captured from the Austrians and Russians at Austerlitz.

A quick walk up the Rue de la Paix—a slow one might prove ruinous to your budget —takes you past jewellers, goldsmiths and furriers to the

Opéra, the massive epitome of the pretensions of Napoleon III's Second Empire. Started at the height of his power in 1862 (by architect Charles Garnier), when Paris claimed to be Europe's most glamorous capital, the Opéra was not completed until 1875. Its neo-baroque style is less of an aesthetic joy than a splendid act of conspicuous consumption proclaiming the triumph of the French bourgeoisie. It takes honours as the world's largest theatre, though it seats only 2,000 people.

The **grands boulevards** leading from the Opéra to the Madeleine are perhaps less fashionable than in their heyday at the turn of the century, but their bustle and great open sweep make it easy to recapture the atmosphere. On the Boulevard des Capucines you will be retracing the footsteps of Renoir, Manet and Pis-

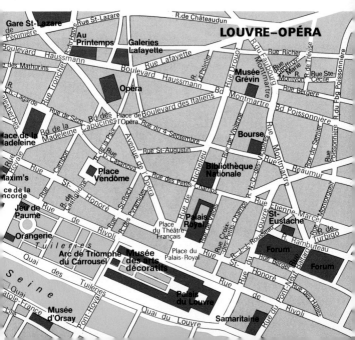

sarro, who took their paintings to the house of photographer Nadar, at number 35, for the first exhibition of Impressionist painting in 1874. The boulevards are now appropriately the home of the town's most popular cinemas—appropriately because it was here at the Hôtel Scribe, that the

Lumière brothers staged the first public moving-picture show in 1895.

Many people are surprised to learn that the **Madeleine** is a church—and, in fact, it did not start out as one. Originally there *was* going to be a church here, and Louis XV even laid its first stone in 1764, but the Revolution halted construction. Then Napoleon decided to put up a huge temple-like structure, Greek on the outside and Roman on the inside. It

In Montmartre, the artist must also be adept at making a deal.

was variously projected as a stock exchange, the Bank of France, a theatre or a state banquet hall. Napoleon himself saw it as a Temple de la Gloire for his military victories until the architect persuaded him to build the Arc de Triomphe instead. After Waterloo Louis XVIII reverted to the plan for a church, but with no transept, aisles or bell-tower, or even a cross on the roof. It remains an awe-inspiring monument embellished on most days by the flower market at its base.

From the Madeleine you can either return to the Place de la Concorde by taking the grand Rue Royale past Maxim's restaurant, a monument no less awesome than the Madeleine, or go up towards the Etoile along the city's most opulent shopping street, the **Rue du Faubourg Saint-Honoré,** with a peek through the gates of the French president's Elysée Palace at number 55. But two other, entirely different neighbourhoods belong to and enrich the Right Bank: Montmartre and the Marais. Each deserves at least a day.

Montmartre

If Paris more than most places thrives on its mythology, few quarters have contributed more than Montmartre, known locally as "La Butte". Long famous as the home of artists and bohemian crazies, it is also a focus of the city's spiritual sources. The pagan and religious aspects of Montmartre's personality begin with the etymology of its name. Scholars still argue whether the popularly accepted derivation of Mons Martyrum, referring to the site of St. Denis's decapitation, is not a pious misconception of the true origins—Mons Mercurii, site of a pagan Roman temple.

A walk around Montmartre will help you make up your own mind. Still topographically the little country village of 400 years ago, it is impossible to drive a car around this area. Take the Métro, Porte de la Chapelle line, that goes from Concorde to Abbesses. (Do *not* get off at Pigalle; however attractive you may find its lurid glitter at night, by day it might depress you into not visiting the rest of Montmartre.)

From the Place des Abbesses, take Rue Ravignan to number 13, Place Emile-Goudeau. This was the site of the Bateau-Lavoir studio, an unprepossessing glass-roofed loft that burned down in 1970. Here—if in any one place—modern art was born: Picasso, Braque and Juan Gris developed Cubism, while Modigliani worked his mysteries and Apollinaire sang it all in the first surrealistic verses.

Properly respectful of the spirits of the past, make your way around the neighbourhood where the illustrious predecessors of these "upstarts" lived and worked—Renoir, Van Gogh, Gauguin—in the Rue Cortot, Rue de l'Abreuvoir, Rue Saint-Rustique (with the restaurant A La Bonne Franquette where Van Gogh painted his famous *La Guinguette*). In artistic terms you move from the sublime to the ludicrous with the street-painters of the old **Place du Tertre.** Too rich a spot to be spoiled by the daubers, this is the very centre of Montmartre's village life, its original public square where marriages werc announced, militiamen enlisted and criminals hanged. You should also visit the Rue Saint-Vincent, site of Paris's own vineyard, the Clos de Montmartre at the corner of the Rue des Saules, where they produce a wine that reputedly "makes you jump like a goat".

At the other end of Rue Saint-Vincent you come around the back of the basilica of the **Sacré-Cœur.** You have probably spotted it a hundred times during the day so its back view will make a welcome change. This weird Romano-Byzantine church enjoys a dubious reputation in the city. The aesthetes quite simply hate its over-ornate exterior and extravagant interior mosaics, or at best find it grotesquely amusing; working-class people of the neighbourhood resent the way it was put up as a symbol of penitence for the insurrection of the 1871 Commune and defeat in the war against the Prussians. The Sacré-Cœur's miraculously white façade derives from the special quality of the Château-Landon stone that whitens and hardens with age. For many its most attractive feature is the view from the dome, which can be visited, covering a radius of 30 miles on a clear day.

Just down the hill from the Sacré-Cœur is **Saint-Pierre-de-Montmartre,** one of Paris's oldest churches. Consecrated in 1147, 16 years before Saint-Germain-des-Prés, it represents a significant work of early Gothic art, belied by its 18th-century façade. The Sacré-Cœur's architect, Paul Abadie, wanted to demolish Saint-Pierre, but he was overruled, and a group of artists succeeded in having it restored, "as a worthy riposte to the Sacré-Cœur".

Every day's walk should end with a good rest, and you should not be put off by the idea of going to the **Cimetière de Montmartre** off the Rue Caulaincourt, a place of delightful tranquillity often neglected for the more illustrious cemetery of Père-Lachaise (see p. 42). You can visit the tombs of Degas, Berlioz, Offenbach, Stendhal, Nijinski and Heine and try to find the excellent bronze sculpture by François Rude at the grave of Godefroy Cavaignac.

Marais

The Marais district, north of the two river-islands, has bravely withstood the onslaught of real estate developers over the years, providing a remarkably authentic record of Paris's development from Henri IV at the end of the 16th century up to the Revolution. Built on land

Crowds flock to the Sacré-Cœur, mainly for its great view of Paris.

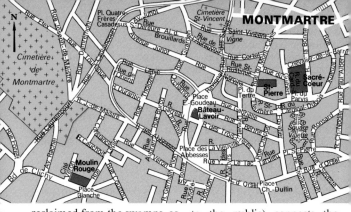

reclaimed from the swamps, as the name suggests, it contains some of Europe's most elegant Renaissance-style houses *(hôtels),* now serving as museums and libraries.

Start at the corner of Rue des Archives and **Rue des Francs-Bourgeois,** named after the poor people allowed to live there tax-free in the 14th century. (Métro line Mairie des Lilas to Rambuteau.) The National Archives are kept here in a magnificent 18th-century mansion, the **Hôtel de Soubise.** The beautiful horse-shoe-shaped *cour d'honneur* leads you into an exquisite rococo world: the apartments of the Prince and Princess of Soubise, the high point of Louis XV decor, contain the Musée de l'Histoire de France.

A garden (not always open to the public) connects the Soubise with its twin, the **Hôtel de Rohan** on Rue Vieille-du-Temple. Be sure to look for Robert Le Lorrain's magnificent stone sculpture, *Chevaux d'Apollon,* over the old stables in the second courtyard. A few steps away, on Rue de Thorigny, you'll find the Hôtel Salé which houses the **Musée Picasso** (see p. 71).

Two other architectural jewels grace the Rue des Francs-Bourgeois—the **Hôtel Lamoignon** at the corner of Rue Pavée and the **Hôtel Carnavalet,** once the home of the illustrious lady of letters Madame de Sévigné and now the Musée Historique de la Ville de Paris (see p. 73).

With a fine dramatic sense, the Rue des Francs-Bourgeois ends at what many consider to be the city's most picturesque square, **Place des Vosges.** Its classical harmony is achieved by a subtle diversity of detail in the gables, windows and archways of its red-brick façades. When Henri IV had the square built in 1605, on the site of a horse-market, it consisted of 36 homes or *pavillons,* each encompassing four arches, nine *pavillons* on each side. But these have since expanded or contracted according to the means of the owners. Place des Vosges remains one of the most luxurious residential areas of Paris. The gardens of the square, now a peaceful playground for children, were a favourite spot

for the aristocratic duel and, after Louis XIII's wedding festivities here, the town's most fashionable promenade.

In those days it was known as the Place Royale. It received its current name for the prosaic reason that the department of the Vosges was the first to pay up all its taxes to the Revolutionary Government. If you are a fan of Victor Hugo, stop by the fascinating **museum** of his manuscripts, artefacts and 350 of his drawings at number 6.

You can finish your visit to the Marais with a walk around the old **Jewish quarter.** Jews have lived continuously on the Rue des Rosiers since 1230,

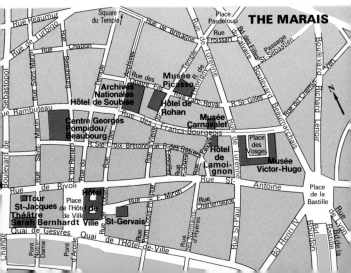

and Rue Ferdinand-Duval was known until 1900 as the Rue des Juifs. Rue des Ecouffes is a lively shopping street, with Jews from North Africa gradually replacing the Ashkenzani of Poland and Hungary who themselves took over from the original Sephardim.

Père-Lachaise

Such is Paris's perpetual homage to the great of its past that the Cimetière Père-Lachaise manages to be an inspiring and quite undepressing pilgrimage for tourists and Parisians alike. This vast "City of the Dead" has a population estimated at 1,350,000 buried since its foundation in 1804. Named after Louis XIV's confessor, a member of the Jesuits who previously owned the land, the cemetery has long been renowned as the resting place for the heroes of the country's revolutions. It even served as a battleground on May 28, 1871, for the last stand of the Communards and a "Mur des Fédérés" marks the place where they were executed by firing-squads at the south-

east corner. In this pantheon of the city's artistic heritage, you will find writers Colette and Alfred de Musset and Italian composer Rossini at lot No. 4, Chopin (11), philosopher Auguste Comte (17), painters Ingres (23), Corot and Daumier (24), La Fontaine and Molière (25), Sarah Bernhardt (44), Bal-

Henri IV made Place des Vosges a lovely place to live. It still is.

zac (48), Delacroix (49), Bizet (68), Proust (85), Apollinaire (86), Isadora Duncan (87), Oscar Wilde (89) (with a fine monument by sculptor Jacob Epstein) and Gertrude Stein (94). Napoleon's emancipation of the Jews meant that they could have their own section, and Napoleon III's deference to the Turkish ambassador for his Eastern foreign policy led to an area for Moslems. Presidents of the Third Republic like Adolphe Thiers and Félix Faure lay just a stone's throw from the radicals they bitterly opposed. Père-Lachaise remains a unique site of national unity and reconciliation.

The Islands

Ile de la Cité

Shaped like a boat with the Square du Vert-Galant as its prow, the Ile de la Cité is the veritable cradle of the city of Paris, the original dwelling place of the fishermen and bargees of early Lutetia. The island also exemplifies what over-ambitious, wilful urban planning can do to charming neighbourhoods. In the middle of the 19th century, the much praised but often insensitive Baron Haussmann swept away nearly all of the medieval and 17th-century structures, leaving only the Place Dauphine and the Rue Chanoinesse (ancient home of the cathedral canons) as evidence of the island's rich residential life.

The baron was also thinking of replacing the triangular **Place Dauphine's** gracious red-brick, gabled and arcaded architecture with a neo-Grecian colonnaded square. But, fortunately, he was forced out of office for juggling his books before the wreckers could move in. The *place*, close by the lively Pont-Neuf, was built in 1607 by Henri IV in honour of his son the *dauphin* (later Louis XIII). Sadly only the houses at number 14 and 26 are still in their original state since 18th-century property developers found it more profitable to remodel the premises.

The massive **Palais de Justice,** today a complex of buildings encompassing the centralized legal machinery of modern France, holds echoes of the nation's earliest kings, who dwelt here, and of the later nobility, aristocracy and Revolutionary leaders, who were imprisoned here before execution. It also conceals a Gothic masterpiece, the **Sainte-Chapelle.** With its walls of stained-glass and its harmonious proportions (nearly equal height and length), the chapel has an ethereal quality—in startling counterpoint to the ponderous surrounding palace. It was built in 1248 by the pious King Louis IX (known as St. Louis) for the relics obtained from the emperor of Constantinople. There are in fact two chapels, the lower for the canons, chaplains and other dignitaries of the church, and the upper one for the king and his retinue. The 15 **stained-glass windows** include 1,134 different pieces depicting mainly Old Testament scenes; 720 of them are 13th-century originals.

Between 1789 and 1815, the chapel served variously as a flour warehouse during the

Some of the Métro entrances are masterpieces of Art-Nouveau design.

Revolution, a clubhouse for high-ranking dandies and finally as an archive for Napoleon's Consulate. It was this latter role that saved the chapel from projected destruction, because the bureaucrats did not know where else to put their mountains of paperwork.

These days they find space in the endless corridors of offices in the Palais de Justice and the nearby Préfecture de Police. What started off in 360 as the site of Julian's coronation as Emperor of Rome, later housing Merovingian kings Clovis, Childebert, Chilpéric and Dagobert, is now strictly "Maigret" country. The great Salle des Pas-Perdus is worth a visit for a glimpse of the lawyers, plaintiffs, witnesses, court-reporters and hangers-on waiting nervously for the wheels of French justice to grind into action.

But their anxiety is nothing compared with those who were condemned to bide their time in the prison of the **Conciergerie** (reached from the Quai de l'Horloge). After April 6, 1793, when the Revolutionary Terror was in full swing, the Conciergerie (named after the royally appointed *concierge* in charge of common-law criminals) truly became the "antechamber of the guillotine". In the Galerie des Prisonniers, Marie-Antoinette, Robespierre, Saint-Just and Danton all spent their last nights after the Revolutionary tribunals had pronounced sentence. The Salle des Girondins displays one of the guillotine blades, the crucifix to which Marie-Antoinette prayed before execution and the lock from Robespierre's cell. Look out on the Cour des Femmes and see where husbands, lovers, wives and mistresses were allowed one last tryst before the tumbrels came. About 2,500 victims of the Revolutionary guillotine passed their final hours in the Conciergerie.

The site of the cathedral of **Notre-Dame de Paris** has had a religious significance for at least 2,000 years. In Roman times a temple to Jupiter stood here; some stone fragments of the early structure, unearthed in 1711, can be seen in the Cluny Museum (see p. 73). In the 4th century the first Christian church, Saint-Etienne, was built here, joined two centuries later by a second church, dedicated to Notre Dame. Norman invasions of Paris left the two edifices in a sorry state and

the Bishop Maurice de Sully authorized construction of a cathedral to replace them in 1163. The main part of Notre-Dame took 167 years to complete and the transition it represented from Romanesque to Gothic has been called a perfect expression of medieval architecture. One dissenting voice was that of St. Bernard, who protested that the godly virtue of poverty would be insulted by the erection of such a sumptuous structure. And some architectural purists today find Notre-Dame a bit "too much". But it was built to inspire awe.

Old Baron Haussmann comes in for criticism again, because he greatly enlarged the *parvis*, or square, in front of the cathedral, thereby diminishing, it is said, the grandiose impact of the western façade. Others argue this brought back the animated street-life of the square, recapturing some of the gaiety of the Middle Ages when the *parvis* was used for public executions and the populace was invited to throw old fruit and rotten eggs provided by the authorities.

The cathedral remains an

In Paris's old quarters, *a bike is often the best way to get around.*

impressive monument, truly the nation's parish church. It has witnessed, in 1239, Louis IX walking barefoot with his holy treasure, Christ's crown of thorns (before the Sainte-Chapelle was built); in 1430, the humiliation of having Henry VI of England crowned King of France; in 1594, Henri IV attending the mass which sealed his conversion to Catholicism and reinforced his hold on the French throne; in 1804, Napoleon's coronation as emperor, attended by the pope but climaxed by Napoleon crowning himself; and in our own day, the state funerals of military heroes such as Foch, Joffre, Leclerc and de Gaulle.

Given the cathedral's gigantic size, the balance of its proportions and the harmony of its façade are nothing short of miraculous. The superb central **rose window,** encircling the statue of the *Madonna and Child*, depicts the Redemption after the Fall. Look for the **Galerie des Rois** across the top of the three doorways. These 28 statues representing the kings of Judah and Israel were pulled down during the Revolution because they were thought to be the kings of France (later restored).

Inside, the marvellous lighting is due in large part to two

more outsize rose windows dominating the transept. Don't miss the lovely 14th-century **Virgin and Child** that bears the cathedral's name, Notre-Dame de Paris, to the right of the choir entrance.

The original architect is anonymous but the renowned Pierre de Montreuil was

responsible for much of the 13th-century work. For the present structure with its majestic towers, spire and breathtaking flying-buttresses, we must be grateful to Eugène Viollet-le-Duc, who worked centimetre by centimetre over the whole edifice between 1845 and 1863, restoring the cathe-

Notre-Dame cathedral, a national shrine of incomparable beauty, sits proudly on the island in the middle of the Seine where Paris was born.

dral after the ravages of the 18th century. For once, it was pre-Revolutionary meddlers—who tried to redecorate and improve—more than the Revolutionaries who where to blame. In 1831, Victor Hugo's novel, *Notre-Dame de Paris* started a public outcry that led to the restoration of the national shrine.

All the original bells have disappeared except for the *bourdon*, dating from 1400, in the South Tower. Its much admired purity of tone was achieved in the 1680s when the bronze bell was melted down and mixed with the gold and silver jewellery donated by Louis XIV's aristocracy. Today it is no longer operated by a hunchback but by an electric system installed in 1953.

Ile Saint-Louis

Very much a world apart, the Ile Saint-Louis is an enchanted, self-contained island of gracious living, long popular with Paris's affluent gentry. President Georges Pompidou lived here (on the Quai de Béthune) and loved to come here from the Elysée Palace as often as possible.

Appropriate to the island's stylish reputation, its church, the **Saint-Louis-en-l'Ile,** is as elegant as one of its great mansions, bright and airy with a golden light illuminating a veritable museum of Dutch, Flemish and Italian 16th- and 17th-century art and some splendid tapestries from the 12th century.

The most striking of the mansions, the **Hôtel Lauzun** at 17 Quai d'Anjou, was built in the 1650s by the great architect Louis Le Vau, who also worked on the Seine façade of the Louvre and Versailles. The Hôtel Lauzun's opulently ornamental decor was to provide a perfect setting for the Club des Haschischins frequented by Théophile Gautier and Charles Baudelaire.

The **Hôtel Lambert,** another impressive 17th-century mansion designed by Le Vau, stands on the corner of Rue Saint-Louis-en-l'Ile. Voltaire once enjoyed a tempestuous love affair here with the lady of the house, the Marquise du Châtelet.

But perhaps the island's greatest pleasure consists in walking along the poplar-shaded streets to the western end of Quai d'Orléans. There you have the most magnificent **view** of the apse of Notre-Dame, which incorrigible romantics much prefer to the cathedral's "front".

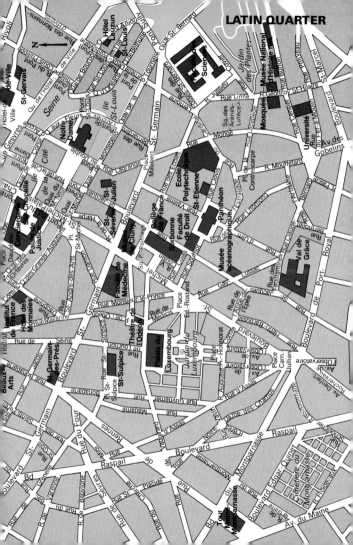

LATIN QUARTER

Left Bank
(Rive Gauche)

Latin Quarter

To get an idea of what the Left Bank is all about, start at the Quartier Latin. Here, facing Notre-Dame, the spirit of inquiry has traditionally been nurtured into protest and outright revolt before subsiding into a lifelong scepticism, as the rebels graduate from the university and move west to the more genteel Faubourg Saint-Germain. Starting in the 13th century, when the city's first "university" moved from the cloisters of Notre-Dame to the Left Bank, the young came to the *quartier* to learn Latin.

In those days *l'université* meant merely a collection of people—students who met on a street corner, in a public square or a courtyard to hear a teacher, standing on a bench or at an upstairs window or balcony, lecture them. Today there are classrooms, overcrowded, but the tradition of open-air discussion continues, often over an endlessly nursed coffee or glass of wine at a café terrace on the Boulevard Saint-Michel or in the streets around the faculty buildings, or in the ever-present cinema queues.

Begin at the **Place Saint-Michel,** where the Paris students come to buy their textbooks and stationery but the young of other countries come to sniff the Latin Quarter's mystique around the bombastic 1860s fountain by Davioud. Plunge into the narrow streets of the Saint-Séverin quarter—to the east Rue

Saint-Séverin, Rue de la Harpe, Rue Galande—into a medieval world updated by the varied exotica of Tunisian pastry shops, smoky Greek barbecue and stuffy little cinemas. A moment's meditation in the exquisite 13th–15th-century Flamboyant Gothic church of Saint-Séverin, where Dante is

Advocating a Left Bank revolution doesn't rule out getting a suntan.

said to have prayed, and you are ready to confront the Latin Quarter's citadel, the **Sorbonne.**

Founded in 1253 as a college for poor theological students by **53**

Robert de Sorbon, Louis IX's chaplain, the university was taken in hand by Cardinal Richelieu, who financed its reconstruction (1624–42). The Sorbonne's church houses the cardinal's tomb, and a memorial service is held for him every December 4 on the anniversary of his death. Visit the Grand Amphithéâtre, which seats 2,700, with its statues of Sorbon, Richelieu, Descartes, Pascal and Lavoisier, the great chemist. As you look at Puvis de Chavannes' monumental painting covering the back wall, *Le Bois Sacré*—allegorising Poetry, Philosophy, History, Geology,

Physiology and the rest—try to imagine 4,000 students packed into that hall in May 1968, arguing whether to have the whole thing plastered over. The student revolt against overcrowding, antiquated teaching and bureaucracy and the very basis of the social system made the Sorbonne the focal point of the movement. When police invaded the sanctuary—which for centuries had guaranteed student immunity—the rebellion was on.

Around the corner, as a kind of didactic inspiration for the students on what hard work can achieve, stands the gigantic Neo-classic **Panthéon,** resting place of the nation's military, political and literary heroes. Originally designed as the church of Sainte-Geneviève for Louis XV (1755), it was secularized during the Revolution as a vast mausoleum with the inscription "To our great men, the Fatherland's gratitude". But the Revolutionaries had a hard time deciding who merited the honour. Mirabeau and then Marat were interred and subsequently expelled. Napoleon ended the controversy by turning the Panthéon back into a church. Throughout the 19th century it went back and forth between secular and consecrated status, according to the regime's political colour. Finally Victor Hugo's funeral in 1885, the biggest the capital had seen, settled the Panthéon's status as a secular mausoleum. Hugo was buried there, followed (retroactively) by Voltaire and Rousseau, and then by prime minister Léon Gambetta, socialist leader Jean Jaurès, Emile Zola, inventor of the blind-alphabet Louis Braille, President Raymond Poincaré and many others.

After which, take a break in the **Jardin du Luxembourg.** If you want to picnic in the park (not on the grass), make a detour first to the old street-market behind the Panthéon on the bustling Rue Mouffetard by the tiny Place de la Contrescarpe, old hunting-ground of Rabelais and his spiritual descendants. Despite their 17th-century origins, the Luxembourg Gardens avoid the rigid geometry of the Tuileries and Versailles. The horse chestnuts, beeches and plane trees, the orangery and ornamental pond, best viewed from the east terrace near the Place Edmond Rostand entrance, were a major in-

Life's problems seem less arduous in a café on Boulevard St-Michel.

spiration for the bucolic paintings of 18th-century master Antoine Watteau.

Montparnasse

Montparnasse is where they invented the cancan in 1845, at the now defunct Grande Chaumière dancehall. In the twenties it took over from Montmartre as the stomping ground of Paris's artistic colony, or at least of its avantgarde. American expatriates like Hemingway, Gertrude Stein, F. Scott Fitzgerald, John Dos Passos and Theodore Dreiser also liked the free-living atmosphere and greatly added to the mystique themselves. Today French as well as American tourists point out the places where the Lost Generation found themselves.

Other quarters are known for their palaces and churches; Montparnasse (named after a 17th-century gravel mound since removed) has cafés and bars for landmarks. The Closerie des Lilas, a centre for French Symbolist poets at the turn of the century, served as a meeting-place for Trotsky and Lenin before World War I and for Hemingway and his friends after the war; the Select, first all-night bar to open in Montparnasse, in 1925, quickly became a Henry Miller hang-out;

La Coupole, favourite of Sartre and Simone de Beauvoir, is still going strong, more living theatre than restaurant; breakfast was taken at the Dôme for a change of air; the Rotonde, favoured by Picasso, André Derain, Maurice Vlaminck, Modigliani and Max Jacob, after a spell as a cinema, is now

back as a restaurant, so that just about all, in one way or another, survive along the bustling **Boulevard du Montparnasse.**

There's always something astir in relaxed Jardin du Luxembourg.

The strength of Montparnasse's myth is such that habitués can pretend not to see the 58-floor Tour Maine-Montparnasse office-skyscraper by the railway station.

Names of fame (Baudelaire, Maupassant, Sartre) haunt the **Cimetière du Montparnasse** just behind.

Saint-Germain-des-Prés

Saint-Germain-des-Prés is the literary quarter par excellence, home of the major publishing houses, the Académie française, bookshops and literary cafés, but also a charming neighbourhood for round-the-clock people-watching. In the years following the Liberation it was known as headquarters for Jean-Paul Sartre and his existentialist acolytes, who were dressed, winter and summer, in black corduroy and long woollen scarves. Foreign students abroad would flock here in the 1950s hoping to see the master at work or at least at play. Failing that, there were always the nightclubs off the Boulevard Saint-Germain, where you could listen to "le jazz hot" and smoke your lungs out.

Today the discotheques have replaced the jazz-cellars and existentialism has had its day, if that is not a contradiction in terms. But the easy-going atmosphere of the outdoor cafés continues around the Place Saint-Germain-des-Prés. On the north side you'll find the Café Bonaparte, on the west the famous Les Deux Magots. Both provide ring-side seats for the street-theatre of mimes, musicians and fire-eaters, who collect money in hats, and for the neighbourhood eccentrics who offer their show for nothing. The Café de Flore up the boulevard has remained more relentlessly "intellectual" in atmosphere, perhaps because of its intense, ideologically confusing history. It has successively been the home of the extreme right-wing Action Française group under Charles Maurras in 1899, the Surrealists of Apollinaire and André Salmon in 1914 (they liked to provoke brawls), and then Sartre's existentialists, a peaceful bunch who never got enough sleep to have the energy for fighting.

Saint-Germain also has its more formal monuments. The church of **Saint-Germain-des-Prés,** a mixture of Romanesque and Gothic styles restored last century, has a clock-tower dating back to about 1000. A 17th-century porch shelters 12th-century doorposts.

To the north of the square runs the Rue Bonaparte, past the prestigious **Ecole des Beaux-Arts.** Incorporated in its structure are fragments of medieval and Renaissance architecture and sculpture that

Parisian hardware store is a veritable goldmine for all manner of off-beat kitchen gadgets.

58

make it a living museum. More recently, in May 1968, it turned into a poster-factory when taken over by the students.

On the Rue des Beaux-Arts is the hotel where Oscar Wilde died in 1900, under the assumed name of Melmoth. He used to complain about the "horrible magenta flowers" of the room's wallpaper, saying "one of us has to go"—and now both have. The hotel has redone Oscar's room in what they consider a more fitting style.

The august **Palais de l'Institut de France,** home of the Académie française, is on the Quai de Conti by the Pont des Arts. Designed by Louis Le Vau in 1668 to harmonize with the Louvre across the river, the Institut began as a school for the sons of provincial gentry, financed by a legacy of Cardinal Mazarin. In 1805 the building was turned over to the Institut, which is comprised of the Académie française, the supreme arbiter of the French language founded by Richelieu in 1635, plus the Académie des Belles Lettres, Sciences, Beaux Arts and Sciences Morales et Politiques. The admission of a new member to the Académie française, an honour more exclusive than a British peerage, is the occasion of a great ceremony. Guides to the Institut like to point out the east pavilion, site of the old 14th-century Tour de Nesle. They say that Queen Jeanne de Bourgogne used to watch from there for likely young lovers whom she summoned for the night and then had thrown into the Seine.

The **Palais-Bourbon,** seat of the National Assembly, provides a rather formidable riverside façade for the Left Bank's most stately district—the elegant 7th *arrondissement* with its 18th-century foreign embassies, ministries and noble residences *(hôtels particuliers)*. The Grecian columns facing the Pont de la Concorde were added under Napoleon and belie the more graceful character of the Palais-Bourbon as seen from its real entrance on the south side. Designed as a residence for a daughter of Louis XIV in 1722, this government building can be visited only on written request or as the guest of a deputy. If you do get in, look for the Delacroix paintings on the history of civilization in the library.

The Foreign Ministry next to the *palais,* better known as the

L'Institut de France, prime showplace for intellectual pyrotechnics.

Quai d'Orsay, is more distinguished for its diplomatic language than its architecture (nondescript Louis-Philippe).

If you are more interested in gracious living than supreme power, you will probably agree with those who feel it's better to be prime minister and live at the **Hôtel Matignon** than be president at the Elysée Palace. The prime minister's magnificent residence at 57 Rue de Varenne is just a short walk from the National Assembly.

Its huge private park has a delightful music pavilion much favoured for secret strategy sessions. The same tranquil street, a veritable museum of 18th-century elegance, contains the Italian Embassy, known as the **Hôtel de La Rochefoucauld - Doudeauville** (No. 47), and the Rodin Museum (see p. 74) in the **Hôtel Biron,** No. 77, which served as the home of Rodin, of poet Rainer Maria Rilke and dancer Isadora Duncan.

Invalides–Tour Eiffel

From the quiet intimacy of this area we return to the massively monumental with the **Hôtel des Invalides,** Louis XIV's first vision of grandeur before Versailles and the work of the same architect, Jules Hardouin-Mansart. Picking up an idea from Henri IV, Louis XIV founded the first national hospital for soldiers wounded in the service of their country. In Napoleon's hands it also became an army museum, another celebration of his victories, and still later the supreme celebration of Napoleon himself, when his body was brought back from the island of St. Helena for burial in the chapel.

The awesomely elaborate tomb, set directly under an open space in the Invalides' golden dome, bears Napoleon's body dressed in the green uniform of the Chasseurs de la Garde. It is encased in six coffins, Chinese-box-fashion one inside the other, the first of iron, the second mahogany, then two of lead, one of ebony and the outer one of oak. The monument of red porphyry from Finland rests on a pedestal of green granite from the Vosges. Twelve colossal statues of Victories by Pradier frame the tomb.

The church of **Saint-Louis-des-Invalides** is decorated with the flags taken by French armies in battle since Waterloo. At the entrance to the Invalides are two German Panther tanks captured by General Leclerc

Only pedestrians can appreciate the all-embracing view from the Pont des Arts.

Romance

A bewitching conspiracy that began with the 15th-century poet François Villon and continued with Maurice Chevalier, Gene Kelly and Edith Piaf has made Paris the supreme city of romance. This is the town, they say, where broken hearts come to mend, where faltering marriages perk up and casual friendships grow brighter with the city's enchanted light. There are places ideally suited for a kiss, a poem, an engagement ring, or whatever other madness this town may drive you to.

Ideal places for whispered tenderness include the Rue Berton, a country lane behind Balzac's house that seems a million miles away from the 16th *arrondissement*. No kiss ever failed here. The Jardin du Vert Galant, at the tip of the Ile de la Cité, is imbued with the lusty spirit of Henri IV. On a moonlit night, the view of the Seine from this tree-enclosed triangle is the stuff dreams are made of. A few steps from the bustle of Saint-Germain-des-Prés is Rue Furstenberg's tiny square. Let the gentle lamplight, softened by the shadows of exotic paulownia trees, work its magic.

How can you miss in a city that is love's open and unashamed accomplice?

in the Vosges. The main courtyard contains the 18 cannons of the *batterie triomphale*, including eight taken from Vienna, which Napoleon ordered fired on momentous occasions, which included the birth of his son in 1811. The cannons sounded again for the Armistice of 1918 and the funeral of Marshal Foch in 1929.

The military complex continues with the **Ecole Militaire** and the vast **Champ-de-Mars** where officers have trained and performed military exercises since the middle of the 18th century. In its heyday, 10,000 soldiers passed in review on this expansive parade ground. Horse-races were held here in the 1780s and five world's fairs between 1867 and 1937. In this century it has been a park for the Left Bank's most luxurious residences.

There are monuments and there is the **Eiffel Tower.** Some celebrate heroes, commemorate victories, honour kings or saints. The Eiffel Tower is a monument for its own sake, a proud gesture to the world, a witty structure that makes aesthetics irrelevant. Its construction for the World's Fair of 1889 was an astounding engineering achievement—15,000 pieces of metal joined together by 2,500,000 rivets, soaring 984

Great European Vacations get off to the right start in the city that puts all the delights of Europe at your doorstep, Amsterdam.

For an exciting array of tour brochures, send for KLM's "It all begins in Amsterdam" kit*, today!

NAME _____

ADDRESS _____

CITY _____

STATE _____ ZIP _____

*Available to U.S. Residents only.

The Reliable Airline of the World. **KLM**
Royal Dutch Airlines

feet into the air on a base of only 1,400 square feet. At the time, it was the tallest structure in the world.

At its inauguration the lifts were not yet operating and Prime Minister Pierre-Emmanuel Tirard, aged 62, stopped at the first platform (187 feet high), leaving his Minister of Commerce to go all the way up to the top to present Gustave Eiffel with the Legion of Honour medal. The tower was slated for destruction in 1910 but nobody had the heart to go through with it.

The critics hated it. Guy de Maupassant signed a manifesto against "this vertiginously ridiculous tower," and Verlaine rerouted his journeys around Paris to avoid seeing it (difficult now, almost impossible then). But today it has

The nation's military tradition is on view at the Invalides museum.

become so totally the symbol of Paris that to dislike the Eiffel Tower is to dislike Paris.

The first platform has a restaurant, the second and third, bars. From the top platform you can theoretically see about 40 miles on a pollution-free day. The best time for the **view** is one hour before sunset.

Museums

The Louvre

The collections of the world's most famous museum are housed in the former royal palace. Open from 9.45 until 5 p.m. Closed Tuesdays.

The Louvre is so huge that people are sometimes frightened of going in at all. But you do not have to be an art fanatic to realize that to come to Paris without setting foot inside this great and truly beautiful palace would be a crime. If you do it right, it can be an exhilarating pleasure. First of all, get up very early on a sunny day and walk around its gardens in the Place du Carrousel. Admire the sensual Maillol statuary and then sit on a bench to take in the sheer immensity of this home of France's kings and storehouse of a world's treasures. At the east end is the Cour Carrée, covering the original fortress built by Philippe Auguste in 1190 to protect Paris from river attack while he was away on a crusade. Stretching out from the Cour Carrée (of which you should see Perrault's marvellous colonnade on the east façade) are the additions of François Ier, Henri IV, Catherine de Médicis, Louis XIV, Napoleon and Napoleon III. President Mitterrand's great glass pyramid in the Cour Napoléon completes eight centuries of construction.

The latest addition is designed by American architect I.M. Pei to provide a spectacular modern entrance, together with underground bookshops and cafés, at the centre of corridors leading to the various wings of the museum.

François Ier, the Louvre's first major art collector, acquired four Raphaels, three Leonardo da Vincis and one Titian (portrait of the king himself). By 1793, when the leaders of the Revolution declared the palace a national museum, there were 650 works of art in the collection; at the last inventory, in 1933, there were 173,000. So don't be depressed if you don't see everything.

If you're planning several visits, you might like to concentrate on just one section at a time—the Italian, the French, the Spanish, the Flemish and Dutch, but also the ancient Egyptian, the Greek and Roman.

For an overall view of the collections, we've attempted a first selection:

Egyptian: lion-headed goddess *Sekhmet* (1400 B.C.) and the colossal *Amenophis IV* (1370 B.C.).

Greek: the winged *Victory of Samothrace* and the beautifully proportioned *Venus de Milo*.

Italian: the sculpture of

Louvre visitors debate merits of famous 16th-century French work.

Two Slaves by Michelangelo; Leonardo da Vinci's fabled *Mona Lisa (La Joconde),* but also his sublime *Virgin of the Rocks;* Titian's voluptuous *Woman at Her Toilet* and sombre *Entombment of Christ;* the poignant *Old Man and His Grandson* of Ghirlandaio.

French: Poussin's bittersweet *Arcadian Shepherds;* Watteau's hypnotically melancholy *Gilles* and graceful *Embarkation for Cythera;* Delacroix's *Liberty Guiding the People* and Courbet's piercing study of provincial bourgeoisie, *Funeral at Ornans.*

Dutch and Flemish: Rembrandt's cheerful *Self-Portrait with a Toque,* his beloved *Hendrickje Stoffels,* also portrayed nude in *Bathsheba Bathing;* Van Dyck's gracious, dignified *Charles I* of England; among the scores of "official" Rubens, his tenderly personal *Helena Fourment;* Jordaens' *Four Evangelists* as diligent Dutchmen.

German: a gripping *Self-Portrait* by Dürer; Holbein's *Erasmus.*

Spanish: the uncompromising Velázquez portrait of ugly *Queen Marianna of Austria;* El Greco's powerfully mystic *Christ on the Cross;* Ribera's gruesomely goodhumoured *The Club Foot.*

English: Gainsborough's exquisite *Conversation in a Park;* Turner's *Landscape with River and Bay;* and **Americans** will be delighted to contemplate Whistler's *Mother.*

Beaubourg

The official name of Europe's most spectacular cultural centre is Centre d'art et de culture Georges-Pompidou, shortened to Centre Pompidou (after the French president whose pet project it was). But somehow Parisians have an aversion to naming their major monuments after their political leaders, and so this bright and dynamic monster will probably always be known quite simply as Beaubourg, after the 13th-century neighbourhood surrounding it.

The combination of public library, modern art museum, children's workshop, *cinémathèque,* industrial design centre, experimental music laboratory and open-air circus on the front plaza is the most popular show in town.

After an initial reaction similar to the delight and rage originally provoked by the Eiffel

Beaubourg's avant-garde sculpture continues the Paris tradition of playful fountains.

Tower, people have grown accustomed to the construction's resemblance to a multicoloured oil refinery. The comparison is readily accepted by its architects, Italians Renzo Piano and Gianfranco Franchi and Englishman Richard Rogers, who deliberately left the building's service system visible and colour-coded: red for the transportation, green for the water pipes, blue for the air-conditioning ducts and yellow for the electrical system.

One of Beaubourg's simplest pleasures is just going up the escalators in the long glass tubes that run diagonally from the bottom-left to the top-right-hand corner. Watch Paris unfold in front of your eyes with a stunning view of the city's rooftops—best on the *fourth,* not the fifth floor.

The **Fontaine Tinguely** on the Place Igor Stravinsky evokes the work of the composer, with moving machines by Tinguely and sculptures by Saint-Phalle.

And More Museums*

Though physically part of the Louvre, the **Musée des Arts décoratifs** is a separate museum with its own entrance at 107 Rue de Rivoli. The rich permanent collection includes tapes-

tries, furniture and porcelain, but look out for the fascinating temporary exhibitions featuring great styles and eras of design history such as Jugendstil, Bauhaus and the American fifties. Next door is the new **Musée national des Arts de la mode,** devoted to the decorative art of which Paris is still the world capital, high fashion.

Right across the river, the 19th-century Orsay railway station has been transformed into the **Musée d'Orsay.** This exciting new museum embraces France's tremendous creativity from 1848 to 1914 in the domains of painting, sculpture, architecture and industrial design, advertising, newspapers, book publishing, photography and the early years of the cinema. It also displays the collection of Impressionists and their followers transferred from the Jeu de Paume museum, now used for temporary exhibitions.

On the river side of the Tuileries, the **Orangerie** is best known for its ground-floor rooms decorated with Monet's beautiful *Nymphéas* murals, offering a moment of repose after a hard day's sightseeing. But you should also take a look upstairs at the excellent Walter-Guillaume collection of Cézanne, Renoir, Utrillo, Douanier Rousseau and Picasso.

*Almost all museums close on Tuesdays.

Another recent addition is the long-awaited **Musée Picasso** (5 Rue de Thorigny in the Marais, Métro Saint-Paul). From the private collections of Picasso's heirs, the museum has received over 200 paintings and 158 sculptures, in addition to hundreds of drawings, engravings, ceramics and models for theatre décors and costumes. It also exhibits the artist's personal collection of masterworks by fellow painters Braque, Matisse, Miró, Degas, Renoir and Rousseau.

Housed in the beautifully restored 17th-century mansion, Hôtel Salé, the museum offers a moving portrait of the man, his family, his mistresses and friends, with letters, manuscripts, photo albums, notebooks, his French Communist Party membership card, bull-

Picasso portrayed the turbulence of his private life in the most enigmatic of expressions.

Time for reflection beneath the deflecting facets of the Géode sphere.

fight tickets and holiday postcards.

The **Grand Palais** and **Petit Palais** (between the Champs-Elysées and the Seine) were both built for the World's Fair of 1900 and are now devoted to large-scale exhibitions of the great masters, though the Petit Palais does have some private collections donated to the state, most notably, the Dutuit that includes paintings by Rubens, Teniers and Ruysdael and superb engravings by Rembrandt and Dürer.

The **Musée Guimet,** 6 Place d'Iéna, houses a magnificent collection of Oriental art from India, Indochina, Tibet, Indonesia, Japan and China.

At the **Musée de l'Homme,** devoted as the name implies to man himself, in the Palais de Chaillot, you can look upon the skull of Descartes, inside which

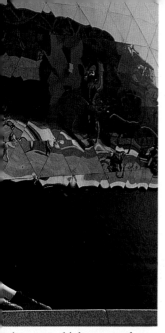

pool on the north side, the *tepidarium* or luke-warm baths on the west side and the *caldarium* or steam room on the south-west side. Even older are the fragments of a monument to Jupiter (probably 1st century A.D.) found near Notre-Dame cathedral. The fine Flamboyant chapel has an admirable Saint-Etienne tapestry, but the most celebrated tapestry in the museum is the world-renowned, 16th-century Boussac series, **The Lady with the Unicorn.**

The later history of Paris is charted in splendid detail at the **Hôtel Carnavalet** located at the corner of Rue des Francs-Bourgeois and Rue de Sévigné (closed on Mondays). This elegant 16th-century mansion —a joy to visit for itself— has a fascinating collection of documents, engravings and paintings of the pomp, circumstance and drama of Paris's history. The outstanding exhibit devoted to the Revolution includes a letter from Robespierre dramatically stained with the author's blood: he was arrested and wounded while signing it.

There are also three delightful small museums devoted respectively to **Balzac** (47 Rue Raynouard), **Delacroix** (6 Rue de Furstenberg) and

the great thinker proved our existence.

The **Musée de Cluny,** 6 Place Paul-Painlevé in the Latin Quarter, is the best place to see the very beginnings of Paris as well as being the city's finest example of Gothic civic architecture. Within its grounds are the remains of the Roman public baths, the **Thermes de Cluny** dating from A.D. 200–300. You can still see the large arched room of the *frigidarium* or cold baths with a swimming

Rodin (77 Rue de Varenne), where you can see how these artists lived as well as admire their work. You'll find the *Thinker* and a bust of *Victor Hugo* in the garden of the Musée Rodin; the house contains the sculptor's private collection of Renoirs, Monets and Van Goghs.

Parc de la Villette

La Villette (on the north-east corner of town, Métro Porte de la Villette) has been converted from the world's biggest slaughterhouse to a striking futuristic complex of cultural and scientific activities.

Refusing to call itself a museum, La Villette's **Cité des sciences et de l'industrie** puts the accent on public participation in all phases of space technology, computers, astronomy and marine biology. The unabashed functionalism of its architecture carries the Beaubourg principle to a logical conclusion. Its most attractive symbol is the shining stainless steel **Géode** sphere containing a revolutionary cinema with a hemispheric screen 36 metres (118 feet) in diameter. There's also a giant rock-concert hall, **le Zénith,** alongside a projected avant-garde musical counterpart to the scientific museum, sorry, city: **Cité de la musique.**

Bois de Boulogne and Bois de Vincennes

To the east and west of the city, but incorporated now into its limits, are the two woods where Parisians take a breather. The **Bois de Boulogne,** more blithely known by residents of western parts of the city as *le Bois,* is the 2,224-acre remainder of the old Rouvray forest left completely wild until 1852. Napoleon III turned it into a place of recreation and relax-

ation for the people of Paris.

The transformations executed by Baron Haussmann were among his happier achievements, and the closest thing Paris has to a London-style park—with roads and paths for cycling and rambles, horse-trails, boating lakes, restaurants and open-air cafés.

One of the main attractions is the Parc de Bagatelle, a walled English garden with the city's most magnificent display of flowers.

Children enjoy the Jardin d'Acclimatation with its miniature train, Punch and Judy show, house of distorting mirrors, pony-rides and a miniature farm of pigs, goats and chickens.

The equally spacious **Bois de Vincennes** on the east offers much of the same attractions, together with France's largest zoo. This former royal hunting-ground has a more popular atmosphere than the Bois de Boulogne.

Paris Underground

One of the most fascinating tours offered by the municipality is through the **sewers.** In perfectly hygienic conditions you can take a guided boat tour underneath the streets (beginning by the Pont d'Alma), while the guide explains how the sewage has been chemically treated and distributed to fields outside Paris for the preparation of fertilizer—ever since 1868. You will notice the network of telegraph and telephone cables, and the old system of compressed-air tubes that was used for sending letters rapidly across Paris.

Another weird underground attraction, for those with a taste for the spooky, is the **Catacombs** (entrance, 2 Place Denfert-Rochereau), a vast network of corridors scooped out under the city to provide building-materials above ground and a mass burial-place down below. The remains of 6 million unidentified dead lay here, transferred from overcrowded cemeteries across the city or buried here in times of mass deaths —like the Revolutionary Terror. Often the bones and skulls are laid out in gruesomely decorative arrangements. Over the entrance to this *ossuaire* are the words of poet Jacques Delille: "Stop, this is the Empire of Death".

What to Do

Shopping

Shopping in Paris is a seductive, exotic adventure that turns adults into children and makes the children wish they had the adults' money. The choice of goods can be overwhelming and the attitude of salesmen and women sometimes forbidding, but if you go into the shop with a clear idea of what you want and a determined air, the aloof stares will melt into charming smiles. A cast-iron rule: never ask for what you want until you have said "Bonjour". (Don't worry if your French is not up to continuing the conversation beyond "Bonjour"; the new generation of sales people in Paris have a good command of English.)

The Big Stores

The department stores best equipped for dealing with foreigners are **Galeries Lafayette** and **Le Printemps,** next door to each other on the Boulevard Haussmann. Both have hostesses to help non-French-speaking customers, as well as the convenience of grouping selections from the major boutiques in their clothes departments. The Galeries has

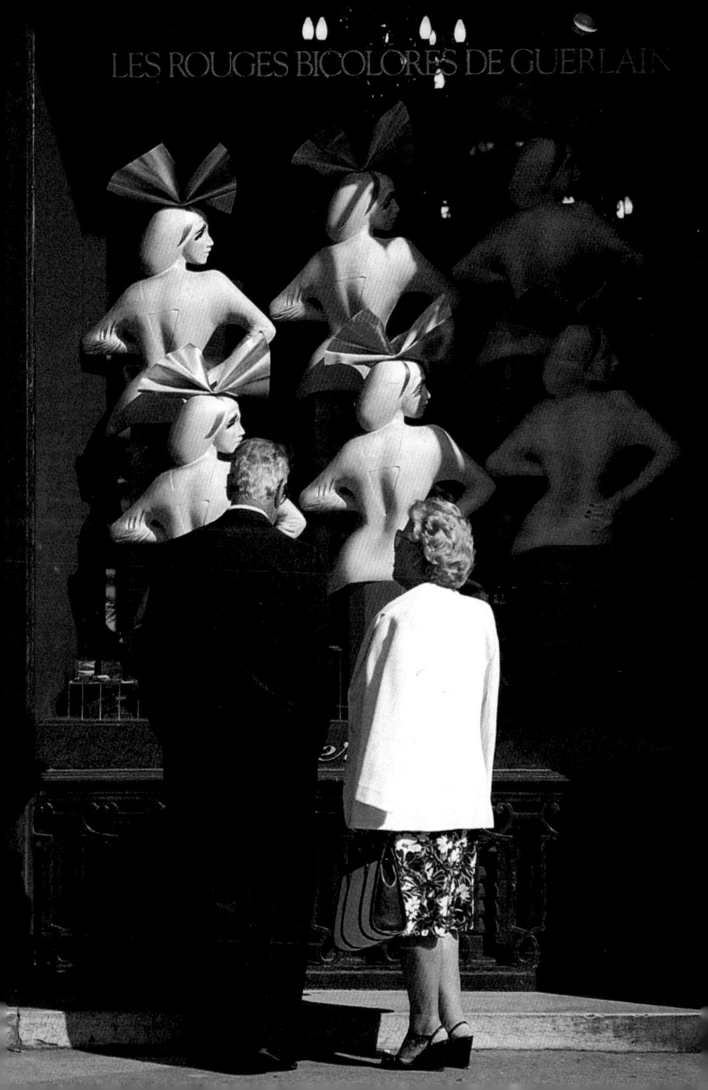
LES ROUGES BICOLORES DE GUERLAIN

lost its great central staircase, but the circular galleries soaring above you still provide the most startling décor of Paris's big stores. They have an enormous chinaware department and excellent perfume and luggage sections. Le Printemps is famous for its lingerie and vast toy department.

For those who like the French habit of dressing up in baker's overalls, waiter's jackets, butcher's aprons, plumber's pants or sewer-worker's waders, the **Samaritaine** department store at Pont-Neuf has an enormous selection of professional uniforms—52 different types representing 52 professions. It also offers a splendid view of the city from its 10th-floor bar.

FNAC, in the younger generation of Parisian department stores (at the Etoile, Montparnasse and the Forum des Halles), has the city's largest selection of books and records.

A strange Parisian phenomenon is **Le Drugstore,** the Frenchman's conception of the American institution of an all-night pharmacy and soda-counter. In French hands it has become a go-go paradise of grocery store, luxury gifts, newsstand, records, books, perfume, electronic gadgets, expensive luggage, car rental, theatre agency—and even a pharmacy—open till 2 a.m. (in Saint-Germain-des-Prés, on Avenue Matignon and the Champs-Elysées). Americans scarcely recognize it.

Fashion

These days, the fashion pendulum occasionally swings to New York, Rome or Tokyo, but the capital for all of them, the showplace for their talent, remains Paris. From the Right Bank, around the Rue du Faubourg-Saint-Honoré, the avenues Montaigne and George-V and over to Place des Victoires and les Halles, the *haute couture* houses and their *prêt-à-porter* (ready-to-wear) boutiques have spilled over to the Left Bank, around Saint-Germain-des-Prés.

Look out not only for the "old school" of Dior, Givenchy, Lanvin, Saint-Laurent, Ungaro and Louis Féraud, but the new generation of Gaultier, Mugler, Montana and their foreign competitors, Yamamoto, Issey Miyake, Valentino and Missoni—as well as the scores of cheaper satellite boutiques that turn out clever variations on the innovators' designs.

For leatherware, Hermès (Rue du Faubourg Saint-Honoré) is an institution all on its own, with high-quality luggage, saddles, stirrups and boots and a much sought-after address-book.

Paris seems to make a great appeal to one's vanity and even visitors get caught up with the desire to look a little better and celebrate with a Parisian hairdo. You can find hairdressing with great flair and style at Alexandre, Carita, Maniatis, Jean-Louis David and Jacques Dessange, most of them with branches on both sides of the river.

Bargains galore in Paris flea-markets, from superb antiques to delightful junk.

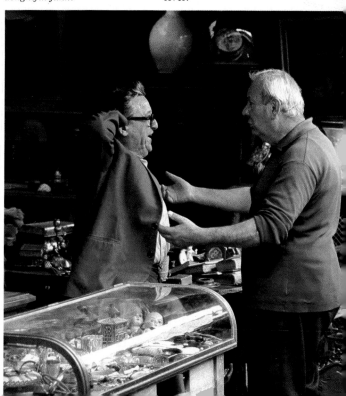

Old and Not-So-Old

Antique-hunting in Paris takes place on two levels—the high-priced shops grouped mainly in the 6th and 7th *arrondissements* on the Left Bank and the flea markets around the city limits. Antiques from ancient Egyptian and Chinese through pre-Columbian to Louis XV, Second Empire, Art Nouveau and Art Déco can be found in elegant or poky little shops between the Quai Voltaire and Boulevard Saint-Germain, on the Rue Bonaparte, Rue des Saints-Pères, Rue de Beaune and Rue du Bac as you walk away from the river and then zigzag the cross-streets of Rue de Lille, de Verneuil, de l'Université and Jacob. You'll find the biggest collection of antique shops in Europe (250 boutiques) at the Louvre des Antiquaires, 2, Place du Palais Royal, open every day except Monday.

The week-end **flea markets** are a well-established Parisian institution. The Marché aux Puces de Saint-Ouen at the Porte de Clignancourt groups half a dozen markets (also open Monday). Vernaison specializes in musical instruments, lead soldiers, old toys, buttons, brass and tinware; Biron has mostly antiques, not differing greatly in price from the Left Bank antique shops; Malik is a great favourite with the young for its Belle Epoque dresses, First World War military uniforms, 1920s hats, and an amazing assortment of Americana; Paul Bert might have that undiscovered masterpiece every flea market goer dreams of—but get there early, practically at dawn, before the professional antique dealers begin rummaging among the unloading trucks; Jules Vallès is the smallest and cosiest, especially good for Art Nouveau lamps, military souvenirs, theatre costumes and old dolls.

The **bouquinistes** (second-hand book sellers) along the Seine—principally from the Place Saint-Michel to the Pont des Arts—are better now for old periodicals than for old books, with a strange nostalgia in the latter for the period of the German Occupation. If you are looking for old books on Paris itself, your best bet is Francis Dasté, Rue de Tournon. For the homesick, a good selection English and American books can be found at Galignani and W.H. Smith on the Rue de Rivoli and at Brentano's on the Avenue de l'Opéra.

Modern Art lovers will find galleries to their hearts' content in Boulevard Saint-Germain and the streets off it.

For a whiff of the country, drop by the Ile de la Cité's flower market.

Gourmet Shops

Paris, more than most cities, is a place from which to take **food** home as a souvenir. Modern packaging makes it easier to transport goods that pre-viously spoiled en route and many stores are equipped to export your purchases for you. The most famous luxury gro-cery shop is Fauchon, Place de la Madeleine. Despite the aristocratic reputation of these shops, the service is friend-ly, courteous and multilingual. Salespeople only become (mild-

ly) annoyed if you suggest they might not have what you are looking for. Of equally high standard but less comprehensive is Hédiard, on the other side of the Place de la Madeleine, which some people prefer for its more intimate, almost 19th-century atmosphere. For the best *foie gras,* perfectly canned for transportation, and for marvellous sausages, hams and other *charcuterie,* try Coesnon, Rue Dauphine.

You may also want to take home some **wine.** The best bargains are at the Nicolas chainstores—150 branches in Paris. The greatest selection is at Legrand, Rue de la Banque (bankers and stockbrokers are notorious connoisseurs). The most intriguing wine-shop is perhaps Caves de la Madeleine, 24 Rue Boissy d'Anglas, where an Englishman holds wine-tasting sessions.

Finally there are the markets—all over town—but particularly colourful on the Rue Mouffetard, Place Maubert and Rue de Seine on the Left Bank and Rue des Martyrs and Avenue du Président-Wilson on the Right Bank.

Man cannot live by bread alone—but a baguette *is more than bread.*

Sports

As the back-to-nature movement gains ground, hitherto blasé Parisians are increasing their interest in sports and *le jogging* or *le footing, le squash* and *le bowling* are winning new adherents. The Bois de Boulogne and de Vincennes are favourite spots for **joggers;** more challenging is the hilly Parc Montsouris. Others trot along the Seine on the non-highway stretches of the Left Bank between Pont-Neuf and Pont Royal.

You can play **tennis** on public courts by contacting the Fédération Française de Tennis (Stade Roland Garros, 2 Av. Gordon-Bennett), or resorting to the jungle law of first-come-first-served at the Luxembourg Gardens' public courts. There are also over 400 clubs to which some hotels have access for their guests.

Swimming is a pleasant joke at the Piscine Deligny, a freshwater pool on the Seine near the Palais-Bourbon, where sunbathers go in minimal costume. More serious action takes place at the Olympic-size indoor pool of the Centre de Natation, 34 Boulevard Carnot, or in one of the 30 other good municipal facilities.

Skating is possible from **83**

September until May at the Palais de Glace, Rond-Point des Champs-Elysées; Patinoire Olympique, Rue du Commandant-Mouchotte; and Patinoire Molitor, Avenue de la Porte-Molitor.

In spectator sports, pride of place goes to **horse racing.** Longchamp and Auteuil in summer are every bit as elegant as Britain's Ascot. The serious punter who wants to avoid the frills and champagne can have a very good time at Vincennes at the trotting races. Betting also takes place in town at the Pari-Mutuel desks of the corner *café-tabac*.

Football and rugby can be seen at the modern flying-saucer-like stadium of Parc-des-Princes and tennis at Roland-Garros, both in the Bois de Boulogne. The palatial Palais Omnisports de Paris-Bercy was designed for a variety of sports.

Excursions

Any excursion outside Paris must include **Versailles** (21 km.), where Louis XIV created the most sumptuous royal court Europe had ever seen, partly for his own glory and partly to keep his nobles in impoverished dependency and away from the intrigues of that trouble-making city of Paris. Architects Louis Le Vau and Jules Hardouin-Mansart and landscape-designer André Le Nôtre began their huge undertaking in 1661. It was completed 21 years later. After the Revolutionary ravages, it became a historic museum in 1832 and was restored in this century. (Closed on Mondays.)

One of the principal attractions of the château is the **Galerie des Glaces.** Here the peace treaty of World War I was signed in 1919. The most impressive façade is in the west, facing the gardens. Try to be there at 3.30 p.m. when the fountains begin to play (three Sundays a month from May to September). You should also see the **Grand Trianon,** the little palace that Louis XIV used to get away from the château, the **Petit Trianon** that Louis XV preferred, and the **Hameau** or "cottages" where Marie-Antoinette went to get away from everything.

You might like to venture further afield to the magnificent Gothic cathedral at **Chartres** (95 km. from Paris), which has the finest stained-

84

Chartres stained-glass windows: a symphony in blue.

glass windows in France, or to the château at **Rambouillet** (54 km.), the summer residence of the French president, where heads of state get together to lament the price of petrol in the beautiful park. An hour's drive north of Paris is the lovely **Forêt de Compiègne** (76 km.), perfect for a cool walk and picnic. You can rent horses at the village of SAINT-JEAN-AUX-BOIS in the middle of the forest and visit the famous clearing in the north-east corner where the armistice was signed in a sleeping-car in 1918—the same sleeping-car that Hitler forced the French to use to sign their capitulation in 1940. A replica of it stands there with a little museum marking the events.

Other nearby sights include the early Gothic basilica of **Saint-Denis** (4 km. from Paris) with royal tombs from the Middle Ages and Renaissance, the national ceramic workshops and museum of **Sèvres** (12 km.), the elegant château and racing course of **Chantilly** (42 km.), **Senlis** (44 km.), where you will find yet another beautiful Gothic cathedral, and the famous forest and château of **Fontainebleau** (65 km.).

The château gardens at Versailles
86 *are a miracle of French precision.*

Entertainment

The Paris night-scene has lost none of the glitter and bounce that Toulouse-Lautrec made famous at the turn of the century. The myth he created in that Belle Époque has sustained itself over the years, and visitors are surprised to discover that his Moulin Rouge, on Place Blanche, still puts on one of the great, boisterous **floor shows** of Europe. The rest of Pigalle is indeed sleazy, but it always was. Taste may have changed over the years but Pigalle has always managed to plumb its lower depths with a certain glee that continues to

hold an almost anthropological fascination for visitors. Bright exceptions remain Chez Michou (Rue des Martyrs), a witty cabaret of talented transvestite impersonators, and two music-halls that launched the careers of Josephine Baker, Maurice Chevalier, Fernandel and Mistinguett—the Folies-Bergère (Rue Richer) and the Casino de Paris (Rue de Clichy). The other floor-show in the grand tradition of girls with feathers, balloons and little else takes place in the Lido over on the Champs-Elysées. But perhaps the most famous modern-day girl-show, conceived with great choreographic talent and de-

cors in which the girls are dressed only in cunning patterns of light, is in the Crazy Horse Saloon (Avenue George-V).

On the Left Bank there are two floor-shows that combine pretty girls and transvestites in a nonstop riot of pastiche, satire and surprisingly wholesome entertainment at the Alcazar (Rue Mazarine) and Paradis Latin (Rue du Cardinal-Lemoine).

If you would rather do the dancing yourself, a plethora of **discotheques** awaits you— either massive New York-style or chic Parisian. And Paris has some 15 **jazz** clubs, the French

You pay a bit more than the bare minimum to see showgirls of Paris.

taking their jazz seriously. The New Morning (Rue des Petites-Ecuries) attracts all the major American and European musicians, while Le Dunois (Rue Dunois) is a modest, intimate place cultivating the avant-garde. You can hear good mainstream jazz at the Bilboquet (Rue Saint-Benoît), Le Furstenberg (Rue de Buci) and the bars of the Méridien hotel Boulevard Gouvion-Saint-Cyr) and Concorde-Lafayette (Place du Général-Koenig). **89**

Those seeking more serious fare will be delighted by the great revival of the **Opéra.** The Orchestre de Paris has also improved its reputation since the advent of musical director Daniel Barenboim. It is worth going to the hall itself for tickets since agencies add at least 20 per cent to the price and cancellations are returned directly to the hall.

The classical **theatre** maintains its exacting standards for Molière, Racine and Corneille at the Comédie-Française (Rue de Richelieu) and more international works at the Odéon on the Left Bank. Drawing-room comedies and the like find a happy long-running home in the theatres around the *grands boulevards*.

If you feel your French is up to it, visit the tiny *café-théâtres* at which you can sip a drink while watching *chansonniers* in satirical cabaret or an avant-garde play. They are centred around the Marais or Montparnasse. For all of these it is a good idea to consult the excellent weekly entertainment-guides, *Pariscope* and *L'Officiel du Spectacle.*

For many, Paris's most important artistic attraction is not the opera, concerts, theatre or cabaret but the **cinema.** On a typical week you will find over 250 different films playing in town, a record that cineasts claim unequalled elsewhere. Paris is a film-crazy town where directors and even screenplay writers achieve a celebrity equal to that of the stars. To enjoy Paris's cinematic riches you should learn: a) not to be intimidated by queues—there

An Opéra gala—one of the truly
great moments of the Paris season.

are always queues and you nearly always get in; b) the ushers expect to be tipped, it is their only income—one franc minimum; c) not to be surprised by applause, even in the middle of the film—cinema is not just an art here, it is a spectator sport; d) the one franc more for tickets on the Champs-Elysées is often for the air conditioning; e) never overdress in the Latin Quarter.

Perhaps from an excess of civilization or sophistication, for a long time Paris has not been a town to celebrate national or religious holidays in any grand style, but there are two days worth noting: **Bastille Day** (July 14) when you can still find a *bal populaire* in the Marais and working-class *arrondissements* (9th, 10th, 11th, 12th, 13th, 18th, 19th and 20th), usually around the firestation; and **Assumption Day** (August 15) when Paris is totally empty and a sudden quiet heaven.

Wining and Dining

There are some tourists who come to Paris without visiting a single museum or church and who would not dream of "wasting" their time shopping. And yet, they come away with tales of adventure, excitement, poetry and romance—and the feeling they know the city inside out. They have spent their time wining and dining and sleeping in between meals. The onslaught of fast food and snack bars has not staled the infinite variety of Paris's restaurants, *bistrots* and cafés, at which anything from a gorgeous feast to a piquant regional sausage is served in the knowledge that eating and drinking are not just a means of satisfying hunger and thirst.

You can best enter into the spirit of this by devoting one, two or even all your evenings to the delights of good food. Go all the way: aperitif, hors d'œuvre, fish course, meat course, cheese, dessert, brandy and coffee. Back home, weddings and anniversaries may be your only occasion. Here, all you have to celebrate is the city

The only thing that's better than a dozen oysters... is two dozen.

itself. Not to dine well in Paris is not to have been there.*

A Primer for Novice Gourmets
Paris has everything except a cuisine of its own. Instead, you can sample food from almost every region of France. But before sitting down to eat, it's useful to have a few basic notions of French cuisine.

First things first. Forgoing the hors d'œuvre does not necessarily mean that the main course will be served more quickly. Besides, it's worth trying some of the simplest dishes that do work genuinely as appetizers: *crudités*—a plate of fresh raw vegetables, tomatoes, carrots, celery, cucumber; or just radishes by themselves, served with salt and butter; *charcuterie*—various kinds of sausage or other cold meats, notably the *rosette* sausage from Lyon, *rillettes* (like a soft pâté) and *jambon* from Bayonne or Dijon; or *potage*—rich vegetable soup, with a base of leek and potato, or perhaps a *bisque de homard* (lobster).

Fish comes fresh to Paris every day. The trout *(truite)* is delicious *au bleu* (poached ab-

---

* For more about wining and dining in France, consult the Berlitz EUROPEAN MENU READER.

Handling the Waiter

Because French restaurants are regarded as secular temples, tourists sometimes feel they must treat waiters and maîtres d'hôtel like high priests and cardinals. First rule: never be in awe of them. They will not bite. If they bark, bark back. These people are not ogres by nature. They grow testy only when you show you are frightened or aggressive—much like the rest of us, really. You must remember that being a waiter is a respected profession in France, and they like nothing better than for you to call on their expertise.

If you are not satisfied with the wine or the meat is too rare, say so. If you do it with a smile, the waiter will be too surprised to argue. In any decent restaurant, surreptitious tipping to get a table when you have not made a reservation is rarely a good idea. But an extra tip (on top of the 15% in the bill) *after* the meal if you are pleased with your service will be greatly appreciated and get you good service if you return. Amazing how human Parisians can be.

solutely fresh), *meunière* (sautéed in butter) or *aux amandes* (sautéed with almonds). At their best, *quenelles de brochet* (dumplings of ground pike) are simply heavenly—light and airy. The sole and turbot take on a new meaning when served with a *sauce hollandaise*, that miraculous blend of egg yolks, butter and lemon juice with which the Dutch have only the most nominal connection.

For your main dish, expect your meat to be less well-done than in most countries—extra-rare is *bleu;* rare, *saignant;* medium, *à point;* well done, *bien cuit* (and frowned upon). Steaks *(entrecôtes* or *tournedos)* are often served with a wine sauce *(marchand de vin* or *bordelaise)* or with shallots *(échalotes).*

General de Gaulle once asked how one could possibly govern a country with 400 different cheeses. Most of them are to be found in Paris and it would be a crime, in the mere name of your sacred diet, not to try at least the most famous of them—the blue *Roquefort,* the soft yellow-white, crusted *Camembert* or *Brie* (the crust of which you can safely remove without offending true connoisseurs), and the myriad of goat cheeses *(fromage de chèvre).*

Desserts are perhaps the most personal of choices at a meal but you should not miss the chance of a *tarte Tatin* of hot caramelized apples, said to have been invented by mistake by a lady named Tatin who dropped an apple pie upside down on the hotplate when taking it out of the oven. Or *profiteroles,* delicate ball-shaped éclairs filled with vanilla ice-cream and covered with hot chocolate sauce.

If a restaurant offers a *menu* (meaning a special fixed-price meal with appetizer, main course and dessert—not the *carte,* which lists all the establishment's dishes), you can usually save quite a bit by taking it. Look, too, for house wine *(vin ouvert)* served by the *quart* (quarter) and *demi* (half) litre, or bottled by the restaurant. It's always cheaper.

Regional Cuisine

With these pointers as a basic gastronomic "vocabulary", you can begin to try out the various regional cuisines to be found around the capital.

Burgundy, the historic cradle of French culinary art, is ideal for those with robust appetites. This wine-growing region produces the world's greatest beef stew, *bœuf bourguignon,* beef simmered in red wine for at least four hours with mushrooms, small white onions and chunks of bacon. Its Bresse poultry is considered France's finest, and the Charolais beef provides the tenderest of steaks. The freshwater fish benefits from another great sauce, Nantua, made with the stock of crayfish *(écrevisses)* and cream. And don't be afraid of the *escargots* (snails). Start with half a dozen and you may find the chewy texture and garlic butter sauce addictive.

Lyon—the gastronomic capital of France, renowned for the quality of its pork, wild game, vegetables and fruit. If you are adventurous, try one of the rich peasant dishes like *gras-double à la lyonnaise,* tripe with onions and vinegar, the famous *saucisson de Lyon* or a succulent chicken *à la crème.*

Bordeaux—the second great wine-growing region and also justly famous for its *bordelaise* sauce, made with white or red wine, shallots and beef marrow, served variously with *entrecôte* steaks, *cèpe* mushrooms or (why not?) lamprey eels *(lamproie).* A surfeit of them may have killed a few medieval kings but the right amount never hurt anyone. The region's Pauillac lamb *à la persillade* (with parsley) is best eaten pink *(rose).*

Provence—the home of garlic, olives, tomatoes and the country's most fragrant herbs. From the coast between Mar- **95**

seille and Toulon comes the celebrated *bouillabaisse*, a Mediterranean fish stew that might contain rascasse, chapon, saint-pierre, eel, red mullet, whiting, perch, spiny lobster, crabs and other shellfish, seasoned with garlic, olive oil, tomatoes, bay leaf, parsley, pepper and (not authentic without it) saffron. It is also the home of frog's legs, *cuisses de grenouille,* much easier to digest, with garlic, parsley and butter, than you might think.

Landes, Languedoc, Périgord—the south-west famous for *pâté de foie gras* (goose-liver pâté) and truffles, and for all the richness of the goose and duck, especially the *confit d'oie* or *confit de canard,* made by cooking the bird slowly in its own fat and then keeping it for days, weeks and even months in earthenware jars. This is the base of the *cassoulet* with haricot beans, pork, mutton, small sausages, or whatever, one of the heartiest cold-weather meals imaginable.

Ethnic Restaurants

Like other capitals of the old colonial powers, Paris gives a prominent place to the cuisine of its empire: spicy stews from the Caribbean Antilles, savoury *couscous* from North Africa, and the delicate rice dishes of Indochina.

As a variation on the ubiquitous Chinese restaurants—many of them now quite luxurious establishments around the Champs-Elysées and Les Halles—try the little Vietnamese, Cambodian and Laotian places in the Latin Quarter and the 13th *arrondissement* behind Place de l'Italie. Since the immigration of the "boat people" of the 1970s, this quarter has become a haven for South-East Asians. Their cuisine uses distinctive touches of mint, lemon-grass *(citronnelle)* and ginger, and a great variety of seafoods. Thai restaurants, serving more highly spiced food, are growing in popularity.

The Indians have also made a strong assault on the Parisian palate, going beyond simple curries and tandoori to the grander subtleties of Mughal and Kashmiri cuisine.

To serve Japanese businessmen and tourists—and discerning Parisians—the neighbourhood between the Opera and Rue de Rivoli has filled with expensive high-class restaurants and more moderate, but excellent snack-bars serving *sushi* (raw fish and rice) and *yakitori* barbecue.

Wine

What is for many people the most intimidating of experiences—ordering a French wine—has in fact far fewer rules than you think. If you happen to like red wine more than white, you can safely and acceptably order red with fish; a light Beaujolais, Morgon or Brouilly chilled goes with both fish and meat. And if you prefer white, you can drink dry Burgundy with fish and Alsatian wine with everything, with impunity. Remember, in a Paris restaurant *you* are king. You prefer beer? Go ahead, it goes especially well with Toulouse sausage and Alsatian *choucroute*.

But if you do want a few basic pointers about the classic wines, the Burgundy reds divide easily into two categories, those that can more safely be drunk relatively young—the supple *Côte de Beaune* wines of *Aloxe-Corton*, *Pommard* and *Volnay*—and those that need to

age a little, the full-bodied *Côte de Nuits* wines of *Vougeot, Gevrey-Chambertin* and *Chambolle-Musigny*. The great Burgundy whites include *Meursault* and *Puligny-Montrachet*.

Bordeaux wines have four main regional divisions: *Médoc*, aromatic, mellow red with a slight edge to it; *Graves*, a soft, easy-to-drink red, both dry and vigorous like the Burgundies; *Saint-Emilion*, dark strong and full-bodied; and the pale golden *Sauternes*, sweet and fragrant, the most distinctive of the soft, aromatic whites. The lesser Bordeaux can all be drunk a couple of years old but good ones need five years.

The Loire Valley produces fine dry white wines, such as *Vouvray* and *Sancerre*, and robust reds like *Bourgueil* and *Chinon*. Perhaps the best-known red wine outside Bordeaux and Burgundy is the *Châteauneuf-du-Pape*, produced in the Rhone Valley and truly magnificent when mature. Other very drinkable regional wines include *Côtes du Rhône, Cahors* and the *Riesling, Traminer* and *Sylvaner* of Alsace.

And for a sparkling finish, the nation's pride and joy, from that little area east of Paris between Reims and Epernay: *Champagne*, which they describe as *aimable, fin et élégant*, "friendly, refined and elegant".

A votre santé!

To Help You Order...

Do you have a table?
Do you have a set-price menu?

Avez-vous une table?
Avez-vous un menu à prix fixe?

I'd like a/an/some...

J'aimerais...

beer	**une bière**	menu	**la carte**
butter	**du beurre**	milk	**du lait**
bread	**du pain**	mineral water	**de l'eau**
cheese	**du fromage**		**minérale**
coffee	**un café**	potatoes	**des pommes**
dessert	**un dessert**		**de terre**
egg	**un œuf**	salad	**une salade**
fish	**du poisson**	sandwich	**un sandwich**
glass	**un verre**	soup	**de la soupe**
ice-cream	**une glace**	sugar	**du sucre**
lemon	**du citron**	tea	**du thé**
meat	**de la viande**	wine	**du vin**

... and Read the Menu

agneau	lamb	**huîtres**	oysters
ail	garlic	**jambon**	ham
anchois	anchovy	**langouste**	spiny lobster
andouillette	tripe sausage	**langue**	tongue
artichaut	artichoke	**lapin**	rabbit
asperges	asparagus	**loup de mer**	sea-bass
aubergine	eggplant	**macédoine**	fruit salad
bar	sea-bass	**de fruits**	
bifteck	steak	**médaillon**	tenderloin
blanquette	white	**moules**	mussels
de veau	veal stew	**moutarde**	mustard
bœuf	beef	**mulet**	grey mullet
cabri	baby goat	**navarin**	lamb stew
caille	quail	**nouilles**	noodles
canard, caneton	duck, duckling	**oignons**	onions
cervelle	brains	**oseille**	sorrel
champignons	mushrooms	**petits pois**	peas
chou	cabbage	**pintade**	guinea fowl
chou-fleur	cauliflower	**poisson**	fish
concombre	cucumber	**poire**	pear
côte, côtelette	chop, cutlet	**poireaux**	leeks
courgettes	baby marrow (zucchini)	**pomme**	apple
		porc	pork
coquelet	baby chicken	**potage**	soup
coquilles Saint-Jacques	scallops	**poulet**	chicken
		radis	radishes
crevettes	shrimps	**raisins**	grapes
daurade	sea bream	**ris de veau**	sweetbreads
écrevisse	crayfish	**riz**	rice
endive	chicory (endive)	**rognons**	kidneys
épinards	spinach	**rouget**	red mullet
flageolets	dried beans	**saucisse/ saucisson**	sausage/dried sausage
foie	liver		
fraises	strawberries	**saumon**	salmon
framboises	raspberries	**sole**	sole
frites	chips (French fries)	**sorbet**	water-ice (sherbet)
fruits de mer	seafood	**thon**	tunny (tuna)
gigot (d'agneau)	leg (of lamb)	**truffes**	truffles
haricots verts	green beans	**veau**	veal
homard	lobster	**volaille**	poultry

99

How to Get There

If the choice of ways to go is bewildering, the complexity of fares and regulations can be downright stupefying. A reliable travel agent, up to date on the latest zigs and zags, can suggest which plan is best for your timetable and budget.

BY AIR

Scheduled flights

Paris is served by two intercontinental airports, Roissy-Charles-de-Gaulle and Orly (see also p.104). Average journey time between Paris and Johannesburg is 14 hours, London 1 hour, New York 7 hours (less than 4 hours by Concorde), Toronto 9 hours.

Charter flights and package tours

From the U.K. and Eire: Most tour operators charter seats on scheduled flights at a reduced price as part of a package deal which could include a weekend or a couple of weeks' stay, a simple bed and breakfast arrangement or a combined "wine tour" and visit to Paris. Among the inclusive holiday packages are special tours for visitors with a common interest such as cookery courses, school trips or art.

However, most visitors from the U.K. travel to France individually, either by booking directly with a ferry operator and taking the car, or signing up for inclusive holidays which offer fly-drive and touring or self-catering arrangements.

From North America: ABC (Advance Booking Charters) provide air passage only (from New York, Chicago, Los Angeles and San Francisco to Paris), but OTC (One Stop Inclusive Tour Charter) package deals include airport transfers, hotel, some sightseeing and meals.

Paris is the starting point for many tours of France. Wine tasting, gourmet and cooking tours, as well as tours of the château country are included in package deals leaving from over a dozen major American and Canadian cities, usually on a seasonal basis (April to October) and for periods of from one to three weeks. You can also choose from fly-drive and fly-rail schemes.

From Australia and New Zealand: Package deals for Paris are offered by certain airlines. You can also travel by independent arrangement (the usual direct economy flight with unrestricted stopovers) or go on an air-and-car-hire arrangement.

From South Africa: There are both excursion fares and numerous package deals including Paris among other European sights.

BY CAR

Cross-channel operators offer plenty of special deals at competitive prices; a good travel agent will help you to find the suitable ferry for your destination.

BY BUS

Numerous lines serve Paris from regional cities like Bordeaux, Lyons, or Nice. Regular services also operate from London to Paris (via Calais).

BY RAIL

All the main lines converge on Paris. There is an excellent network of ultra-rapid express trains, TGVs (1st and 2nd class, advance booking compulsory, certain trains with supplement). Auto-train services *(Trains Autos Couchettes)* are also available from all major towns.

The journey from London to Paris takes from 6 to 11 hours by train. British and French railways offer London-to-Paris services with the possibility of overnight carriages from London. From Boulogne hoverport, there's a 2-hour, 20-minute turbo-train service to Paris (Gare du Nord).

Tickets. Visitors from abroad can buy a *France-Vacances Spécial* pass, valid for specified periods of unlimited travel on first or second class, with reductions on the Paris transport network and one or two days free car rental (with first class only), depending on type of card.

The *Rail Europ S* (senior) card, obtainable before departure only, entitles senior citizens to purchase train tickets for European destinations at reduced prices.

Any family of at least 3 people can buy a *Rail-Europ F* (family) card: the holder pays full price, the rest of the family obtain a 50% reduction in France, Switzerland and 13 other European countries; the whole family is also entitled to a 30% reduction on Sealink and Hoverspeed Channel crossings.

Anyone under 26 years of age can purchase an *Inter-Rail* card which allows one month's unlimited 2nd-class travel.

People living outside Europe and North Africa can purchase a *Eurailpass* for unlimited rail travel in 16 European countries including France. This pass must be obtained before leaving home.

When to Go

Paris enjoys a mild Continental climate without extremes of hot and cold. From mid-July to the end of August there seem to be more foreign than French people in Paris and shopkeepers and restaurant owners often close up and go on holiday themselves. The best seasons to visit Paris are spring and autumn. The following chart gives an idea of the average monthly temperature in Paris:

	J	F	M	A	M	J	J	A	S	O	N	D
°C	3	4	7	10	14	16	19	18	15	11	6	4
°F	37	39	45	50	57	61	66	64	59	52	43	39

Planning Your Budget

The following are some prices in French francs (F). However, they must be regarded as approximate and taken as broad guidelines; inflation in France, as elsewhere, rises steadily.

Airport transfers. Bus to Orly 27 F, to Charles-de-Gaulle 34 F. Train (2nd class) to Orly 17.30 F, to Charles-de-Gaulle 23 F. Taxi to Orly approx. 150 F, to Charles-de-Gaulle approx. 200 F.

Baby-sitters. 22–25 F per hour.

Bicycle hire. 190–300 F per week, plus 500–700 F refundable deposit.

Car hire (international company). *Renault 5 GTL* 200 F per day, 2.67 F per km., 2,212 F per week with unlimited mileage. *Renault 11* 244 F per day, 3.69 F per km., 2,996 F per week with unlimited mileage. *BMW 520* 457 F per day, 5.20 F per km., 7,168 F per week with unlimited mileage. Add insurance. Tax included.

Cigarettes. French 4.50–7 F, foreign 7–13 F, cigars 17–48 F per piece.

Entertainment. Discotheque (admission and first drink) 60–110 F, nightclub with dinner and floor show 250–485 F, cinema 30–37 F. Special rates for students/groups/Mondays 20–25 F.

Guides. 525–650 F for half-day.

Hairdressers. *Man's* haircut 80–180 F. *Woman's* cut 80 F and up, shampoo and set/blow-dry 90–150 F, colour rinse/dye 80–220 F.

Hotels (double room with bath). ****L 1,000–1,500 F, **** 600–900 F, *** 350–500 F, ** 250–350 F, * 150–250 F (* without bath, 80–120 F).

Meals and drinks. Continental breakfast, hotel 15–60 F, café 15–28 F. Lunch or dinner (in fairly good establishment) 80–200 F, coffee 5–8 F, beer 8–20 F, bottle of wine 30 F and up, cocktail 30–60 F, whisky 28–60 F, cognac 25–60 F.

Métro. 2nd-class ticket 4.60 F, 10 tickets *(carnet)* 27.50 F for 2nd class, 42 F for 1st class, weekly *carte orange (hebdomadaire)* bought for each Monday through Sunday only (valid on buses and Métro) 43 F (2nd class), monthly *carte orange* (2nd class) 152 F (also valid on buses). "Paris Sésame" card (bus or 2nd-class Métro) 55 F for two days, 83 F for four days, 138 F for seven days.

Sightseeing. Boats 23–25 F, museums 8–25 F.

Taxis. Start at 8.50 F (3.80 F extra at stations and terminals), 2.44 F per kilometre. Night rates are higher.

BLUEPRINT for a Perfect Trip

An A-Z Summary of Practical Information and Facts.

Contents

CONTENTS

Listed after most main entries is an appropriate French translation, usually in the singular. You'll find this vocabulary useful when asking for information or assistance.

AIRPORTS *(aéroport).* Paris is served by two main airports, Roissy-Charles-de-Gaulle, about 15 miles north-east of the city, with two terminals (C.D.G. 2 essentially for Air France flights), and Orly, about 9 miles to the south, with its two buildings, Orly-Sud and Orly-Ouest. Most intercontinental flights use Charles-de-Gaulle, a space-age modular construction. Both airports have currency-exchange banks, excellent restaurants, snack bars, post offices and well-stocked duty-free shops. **A**

There is regular and comfortable bus service between airports and between the airports and Paris. The buses leave every twenty minutes from about 6.00 a.m. to 11.00 p.m. There's service outside of those hours from the terminals in Paris to the airport 45 minutes before airport check-in time. The terminal *(aérogare)* for Charles-de-Gaulle airport is at Porte Maillot, near the Etoile. Orly is served by the Invalides terminal. Average time to the airports from these terminals is around 40 minutes; it takes an hour and a quarter to get from one airport to the other by bus. You should plan to leave early if you travel during peak traffic hours.

You can also reach the airports by rail at a very modest price. Trains leave every 15 minutes from about 5 a.m. to 11 p.m. and take 45–75 minutes from the Gare du Nord to Charles-de-Gaulle. From Quai d'Orsay, Saint-Michel or Austerlitz stations to. Orly the trip takes 40–60 minutes. Trains leave frequently from early morning to late at night. See p. 103 for rates.

There is also a regular helicopter service between airports and Paris. The Héliport de Paris is situated at 4, avenue de la Porte de Sèvres in the south-west (Métro Balard).

From the arrivals hall of Charles-de-Gaulle airport, you can contact free a broad selection of hotels throughout the city. By pressing a button, a lamp lights on a map showing position of hotel and prices; by pressing a second one, you get into direct telephone contact with the hotel. The reservation will be kept for you for up to two hours following your call.

Where's the bus/train for...?   **D'où part le bus/le train pour...?**   **105**

B **BANKS and CURRENCY-EXCHANGE OFFICES** *(banque; bureau de change)*. Hours vary, but most Paris bank are open from 9 a.m. to 4.30 p.m., Mondays to Fridays. A few banks and currency-exchange offices operate later and on weekends. The Paris Tourist Information Office can provide a list of these.

Your hotel will usually change currency or traveller's cheques into francs, but the rate is not favourable. Always take your passport when you change money.

I want to change some pounds/ dollars.	**Je voudrais changer des livres sterling/dollars.**

BUS SERVICE *(autobus)*. Bus transport around Paris and the suburbs is efficient, though not always fast. Stops are marked by red and yellow signs, with bus numbers posted. Most buses run from 7 a.m. to 8.30 p.m., some to 12.30. Service is reduced on Sundays and holidays. You use one, two or three tickets depending on the distance. You can buy a ticket as you board the bus. But for frequent bus travel it's less expensive to use one or two tickets from a series *(carnet)* purchased in Métro stations, special two-, four- or seven-day tourist passes or the *carte orange* (see MÉTRO). Bus and Métro tickets are interchangeable.

Do you go to…?	**Est-ce que vous allez à…?**

C **CAR HIRE** *(location de voitures)*. All car-hire firms in Paris handle French-made cars and often foreign makes. Local firms sometimes offer lower prices than the big international companies, but you may have to turn the car in at the same place, rather than dropping it off in another town. See sample rates on p.103. Ask for any available seasonal deals.

To hire a car you must furnish a valid driving licence (held for at least one year) and your passport. Depending on the model you rent and the hiring firm, minimum age for renting a car varies from 21 to 25. Holders of major credit cards are normally exempt from advance deposit payments; otherwise you must pay a substantial (refundable) deposit for a car.

I'd like to hire a car tomorrow.	**Je voudrais louer une voiture demain.**
for one day/a week	**pour une journée/une semaine**
Please include full insurance.	**Avec assurance tous risques, s'il vous plaît.**

CHILDREN. The younger set will find a lot to do in Paris. The Eiffel Tower and boat trips are good fun for everyone. Paris's main zoo (open daily from 9 to 5.30) is in the Bois de Vincennes, easily reached by Métro. The Jardin d'Acclimatation of the Bois de Boulogne is a very special games-and-zoo park, complete with pony rides, marionette shows and other diversions. Prices are reasonable, and children love it (open from 9.30 to 6.30 every day). There are also art workshops for kids on Wednesday and Saturday afternoons in the Centre Georges Pompidou, Plateau Beaubourg (tel. 42.77.12.33). Ask for the Atelier des Enfants.

Reputable student and service organizations can provide babysitters *(babysitter, garde d'enfant)*. Ask at your hotel or the tourist office. You should try to request a sitter at least a day ahead. For prices, see p. 103.

Can you get me a babysitter for tonight/tomorrow night?	**Pouvez-vous me trouver une baby-sitter pour ce soir/demain soir?**

CIGARETTES, CIGARS, TOBACCO *(cigarettes; cigares; tabac).* Tobacco is a state monopoly in France, and the best place to buy your cigarettes is at an official *débit de tabac* (licensed tobacconist). There are plenty of these—cafés and bars and many newsagents—bearing the conspicuous double red cone.

French cigarettes include brands with dark or light tobacco, with or without filter. Dozens of foreign brands are also available at higher prices (see p. 103).

A packet of.../A box of matches please.	**Un paquet de.../Une boîte d'allumettes, s'il vous plaît.**
filter-tipped/without filter	**avec/sans filtre**
light/dark tobacco	**du tabac blond/brun**

CLOTHING *(habillement).* The world's fashion capital is a varied show on the streets. Women feel at home in anything from classic suits to the latest zany mode or jeans. Discretion and practicality are the rule. Paris women don't dress up much in the evening, though you'll want a cocktail dress or dressy slacks and blouses for better restaurants, nightclubs and discothèques.

Some restaurants require jacket and tie for men; and you'll probably get better service at most hotels and restaurants in conservative dress.

Unpredictable continental weather requires a versatile wardrobe, though neither in summer or winter are you likely to meet extremes. For **107**

summer a good rule is lightweight clothing with a warm sweater or
blazer and a raincoat. In winter, too, a raincoat is sometimes necessary,
plus light woollen clothes and a warm coat and boots for the coldest
days.

COMPLAINTS *(réclamation)*

Hotels and restaurants: Complaints should be referred to the owner or
manager of the establishment in question. Try a firm attitude, and if this
doesn't work you can take more serious steps. In the case of a hotel, you
can consult the trade organization, the Syndicat Général de l'Industrie
Hôtelière, 22, av. de la Grande-Armée, 75016 Paris; tel. 43.80.08.29.

Serious complaints may also be taken to the Préfecture de Police
de Paris, 7–9, bd du Palais, 75004 Paris; tel. 42.60.33.22.

Bad merchandise: Within about 10 days of purchase a store will
usually exchange faulty merchandise (if you have the receipt), but you
will hardly ever get your money back.

Prices: If you wish to complain about a price you consider exorbitant,
phone the Service de la Concurrence et de la Consommation,

8, rue Froissard, tel. 42.71.23.10

I'd like to make a complaint.   **J'ai une réclamation à faire.**

CONVERTER CHARTS. For fluid and distance measures, see p. 111.
France uses the metric system.

Temperature

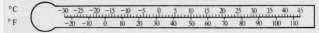

Length

Weight

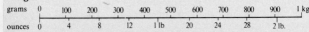

CREDIT CARDS and TRAVELLER'S CHEQUES *(carte de crédit; chèque de voyage, traveller's cheque)*

Credit cards. Most hotels, smarter restaurants, some boutiques, carhire firms and tourist-related businesses accept certain credit cards.

Traveller's cheques. Hotels, travel agents and many shops accept them, although the exchange rate is invariably better at a bank. Don't forget to take your passport when going to cash a traveller's cheque.

Paying cash. Some shops or hotels may accept payment in sterling or dollars but the exchange rate will not be advantageous.

Do you accept traveller's cheques?	**Acceptez-vous les chèques de voyage?**
Can I pay with this credit card?	**Puis-je payer avec cette carte de crédit?**

CRIME and THEFT *(délit; vol).* Paris has its share of pickpockets, so watch your wallet and handbag, especially in crowds. Keep items of value in your hotel safe and obtain a receipt for them. It's a good idea to leave large amounts of money there as well.

Lock your car at all times and leave nothing valuable inside, or put what you're leaving in the locked boot(trunk). Any loss or theft should be reported at once to the nearest *commissariat de police* (see POLICE).

I want to report a theft.	**Je veux signaler un vol.**
My ticket/wallet/passport/handbag/credit card has been stolen.	**On a volé mon billet/portefeuille/ passeport/sac à main/(ma) carte de crédit.**

CURRENCY *(monnaie).* For currency restrictions, see CUSTOMS CONTROLS. The French *franc* (abbreviated F or FF) is divided into 100 *centimes*. Current coins include 5-, 10-, 20- and 50-centime pieces as well as 1-, 2-, 5- and 10-franc pieces. Banknotes come in denominations of 20, 50, 100, 200 and 500 francs.

Could you give me some (small) change?	**Pouvez-vous me donner de la (petite) monnaie?**

CUSTOMS CONTROLS *(douane).* There's no limit on the importation of local or foreign currencies or traveller's cheques. Unless a declaration was made on entry, non-residents are allowed to reconvert no more than 12,000 French francs into foreign currency when leaving the country.

C The following chart shows some main items you may take into France:

Cigarettes	Cigars	Tobacco	Spirits	Wine
1) 400	100	500 g.	1 l.	2 l.
2) 300 or	75 or	400 g.	1½ l. and	5 l.
3) 200	50	250 g.	1 l.	2 l.

1) Visitors arriving from outside Europe
2) Visitors arriving from E.E.C. countries with non-duty-free items
3) Visitors arriving from E.E.C. countries with duty-free items, or from other European countries

For what you can bring back home, ask before leaving home for the customs notice setting out allowances. See also ENTRY FORMALITIES.

I've nothing to declare.	**Je n'ai rien à déclarer.**
It's for my own use.	**C'est pour mon usage personnel.**

D **DRIVING IN FRANCE.** To take a car into France, you will need:

● A valid driving licence
● Car registration papers
● A red warning triangle and a set of spare bulbs

The green card is no longer obligatory, but full insurance coverage is strongly recommended.

Drivers and front-seat passengers are required by law to wear seat belts. Children under 10 may not travel in the front (unless the car has no back seat). Driving on a provisional licence is not permitted in France. Minimum age is 18.

Driving regulations: As elsewhere on the Continent, drive on the right, overtake on the left, yield right-of-way to all vehicles coming from the right (except on roundabouts), unless otherwise indicated. Speed limits are 45 or 60 kph (kilometres per hour) in residential areas of Paris and its suburbs, 90 kph on through roads, 110 kph on dual carriageways (divided highways) and 130 kph on motorways (expressways) called *autoroutes*. When roads are wet, all limits are reduced by 10 kph. The word *rappel* means a restriction is continued.

Driving in Paris is hectic. Stick to your own pace and keep a safe distance between you and the vehicle in front. Be especially wary of vehicles coming from the right.

Road conditions: Beware of traffic jams on the major roads and motorways as you enter and leave Paris, especially on long weekends and around the summer dates of July 1 and 15, August 1 and 15 and September 1. Paris traffic police *(Gardiens de la Paix)* direct traffic and are helpful in giving directions (see POLICE).

Parking: This is a major problem in the capital, which authorities are trying to solve by building new underground parking lots, indicated by a large blue "P". In the centre most street parking is metered. The blue zones require the *disque de stationnement* (obtainable from petrol stations or stationers), which you set to show when you arrived and when you must leave.

Some streets have alternate parking on either side of the street according to which part of the month it is (the dates are marked on the signs). Fines for parking violations can be heavy, and in serious cases your car may be towed away or have a wheel clamp attached until you pay up at the local *commissariat*, or police station.

Breakdowns: It's wise to have internationally valid breakdown insurance, and to ask for an estimate *before* undertaking repairs. Two companies which offer 24-hour breakdown service are Service Dépannage Automobiles, tel. 42.36.10.00 and SOS Dépannage, tel. 47.07.99.99.

Fuel and oil: Fuel is available in super (98 octane), normal (90 octane), lead-free (still rare; 95 octane), and diesel *(gas-oil)*. All grades of motor oils are on sale. Service-station attendants are tipped for any additional services rendered.

Fluid measures

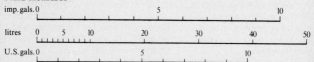

Distance

D **Road signs:** Most road signs are the standard pictographs used throughout Europe, but you may encounter these written signs as well:

Accotements non stabilisés	Soft shoulders
Chaussée déformée	Bad road surface
Déviation	Diversion (detour)
Douane	Customs
Gravillons	Loose gravel
Impasse	Cul-de-sac (dead-end)
Péage	Toll
Priorité à droite	Yield to traffic from right
Ralentir	Slow
Sauf riverains	Entry prohibited except for inhabitants of street
Sens unique	One-way street
Serrez à droite/gauche	Keep right/left
Sortie de camions	Lorry (truck) exit
Stationnement interdit	No parking
Véhicules lents	Slow vehicles

(international) driving licence	**permis de conduire (international)**
car registration papers	**carte grise**
Are we on the right road for…?	**Sommes-nous sur la route de…?**
Fill the tank, please.	**Le plein, s'il vous plaît.**
normal / super / lead-free	**normale / super / sans plomb**
Check the oil / tires / battery.	**Veuillez contrôler l'huile / les pneus / la batterie.**
I've had a breakdown.	**Ma voiture est en panne.**
There's been an accident.	**Il y a eu un accident.**

E **ELECTRIC CURRENT.** You will probably only find 220-volt, 50-cycle A.C. in Paris although some of the oldest hotels may still have 110 volts. British and American visitors using electric appliances from home should remember to buy the necessary adaptors. For razors, just about all hotels have the possibility of both 110 and 220, or the razors themselves do.

EMBASSIES and CONSULATES *(ambassade; consulat).* Contact your embassy or consulate when in trouble (loss of passport, theft or
loss of all your money, problems with the police, serious accident).

Australia	embassy and consulate, 4, rue Jean-Rey, 75015 Paris; tel. 45.75.62.00
Canada	consulate, 35, av. Montaigne, 75008 Paris; tel. 47.23.01.01
Eire	consulate, 12, avenue Foch (enter from 4, rue Rude), 75016 Paris; tel. 45.00.20.87
New Zealand	embassy-chancellery, 9, rue Léonard-de-Vinci, 75016 Paris; tel. 45.00.24.11
South Africa	chancellery-consulate, 59, quai d'Orsay, 75007 Paris; tel. 45.55.92.37
United Kingdom	consulate, 35, rue du Faubourg Saint-Honoré, 75008 Paris; tel. 42.66.91.42
U.S.A.	consulate, 2, rue St-Florentin, 75008 Paris; tel. 42.96.12.02

Where's the... embassy/consulate?	**Où se trouve l'ambassade/ le consulat...?**
I'd like to phone the... embassy.	**Je voudrais téléphoner à l'ambassade...**
American/British Canadian/Irish	**américaine/britannique canadienne/irlandaise**

EMERGENCIES *(urgence)*. You can get assistance anywhere in France by dialling the number 17 for the police *(Police-Secours);* 18 for the fire brigade *(pompiers)*. Paris has an efficient anti-poison centre (tel. 42.05.63.29). You can get advice for other urgent medical problems by dialling S.O.S. Médecins: 47.07.77.77.

Careful!	**Attention!**	Police!	**Police!**
Fire!	**Au feu!**	Stop, thief!	**Au voleur!**
Help!	**Au secours!**		
Can you help me?		**Pouvez-vous m'aider?**	

ENTRY FORMALITIES. See also CUSTOMS CONTROLS and DRIVING IN FRANCE. Visitors from E.E.C. countries and Switzerland need only a valid passport to enter France. If you come from another country, check with the nearest French embassy first to see if you need a visa. Though Europeans and North American residents are not subject to any health requirements, visitors from further afield may require a smallpox vaccination. Check with your travel agent before departure. **113**

G **GUIDES and INTERPRETERS** *(guide; interprète).* The Tourist Information Office provides a list of official guides. The Agence Nationale pour l'Emploi, a public placement service, can usually find you a guide-interpreter at the lowest prices. Telephone 43.55.44.05. "Meet the French" (182, bd Pereire; tel. 45.74.77.12) offers car with chauffeur-guide at a fixed price (excluding museum entry tickets).

Reputable travel agencies also furnish guides and cars, and the larger hotels have lists of chauffeur-guides. For prices see p. 103.

H **HAIRDRESSERS** *(coiffeur).* Prices vary widely according to the class of establishment, but rates are often displayed in the window.

Most *coiffeurs* include service charges in the price, but it's customary to give something. See p. 103 for prices.

Not too much off (here).	**Pas trop court (ici).**
Trim the fringe (bangs)/nape of the neck.	**Coupez un peu la frange/sur la nuque.**
I'd like a perm/blow-dry.	**J'aimerais une permanente/un brushing.**

HEALTH *(santé).* Fatigue, change of diet and over-indulgence (especially in wine) are the main culprits causing the common "tourist's complaint". Watch the drinking and try French mineral water, which helps to digest meals. Serious gastro-intestinal problems lasting more than a day or two should be looked after by a doctor. See MEDICAL CARE.

HOTELS and ACCOMMODATION *(hôtel; logement).* Paris offers a wide range of hotels to suit every taste and budget. Advance bookings are highly recommended, since during holiday season and commercial exhibition weeks, rooms can be almost impossible to find.

Officially, hotels are classified into five categories; a booklet is available at the Paris Tourist Information Office. Rates, fixed according to amenities and the hotel's location, should be posted visibly at reception desks and behind each room door. See page 103 for rates.

Newspapers such as *Figaro* and the *International Herald Tribune* list available accommodation for rent. Most houses and flats are available for long lease only, though some can be let for a month or less. Agencies take large fees, but some flats can be rented from the owner or subleased from the tenant without a fee.

See also YOUTH HOSTELS and under AIRPORTS.

a double/single room with/without bath/toilet	**une chambre à deux lits/un lit avec/sans bains/toilettes**
What's the rate per night?	**Quel est le prix pour une nuit?**
I'm looking for a flat to rent for a month.	**Je cherche un appartement à louer pour un mois.**

HOURS *(heures d'ouverture)*. Although you'll find tobacconists or small shops which sell food and wine open as early as 7 a.m. and as late as midnight, department stores and most shops do business from 9.30 a.m. to 6.30 p.m., Mondays through Saturdays. Boutiques and art galleries often stay open a bit later, especially in the summer.

Watch out for variable lunch hours; businesses and smaller shops close for an hour or so. Banks and some offices close at noon on the day before public holidays. Most museums and monuments open around 10 a.m. and close about 5 p.m. Virtually all are closed on Tuesdays.

See also sections on POST OFFICE, BANKS AND CURRENCY EXCHANGE.

LANGUAGE. You'll usually hear well-enunciated French in Paris, spoken quite quickly. But there are myriad accents, since many Parisians come from the provinces, North Africa or further afield.

Although many Frenchmen speak some English, the French really appreciate a tourist making an effort to speak French, even if it's only the odd word.

The Berlitz phrase book FRENCH FOR TRAVELLERS covers almost all situations you're likely to encounter in your travels in France. In addition, the Berlitz French-English/English-French pocket dictionary contains a glossary of 12,500 terms, plus a menu-reader supplement.

Good morning/Good afternoon	**Bonjour**
Good afternoon/Good evening	**Bonsoir**
Thank you	**Merci**
Please	**S'il vous plaît**
Goodbye	**Au revoir**
You're welcome.	**Je vous en prie.**
Speak slowly, please.	**Doucement, s'il vous plaît.**
I didn't understand.	**Je n'ai pas compris.**

L **LAUNDRY and DRY CLEANING** *(blanchisserie; nettoyage à sec).* If your hotel will not take care of laundry or cleaning, you can have clothes cleaned quickly and cheaply in chain dry cleaners (not recommended, however, for fragile fabrics or difficult spots). Better care takes longer and is more expensive; prices vary according to fabric and cut.

When will it be ready?	**Quand est-ce que ce sera prêt?**
I must have it tomorrow morning.	**Il me le faut pour demain matin.**

LOST PROPERTY *(objets trouvés).* If loss or suspected theft occurs in your hotel, check first at the desk. They may suggest you report the loss to the local police station *(commissariat).* Restaurant and café personnel are quite honest about returning objects left behind; they turn valuables over to the police.

Lost objects usually end up at the Bureau des Objets Trouvés, 36, rue des Morillons, 75015 Paris. If you've lost a passport, check first with your embassy, as the Bureau des Objets Trouvés would transfer it there first. Forms must be filled out in French, though there are usually English-speakers on hand.

I've lost my wallet/handbag/passport.	**J'ai perdu mon portefeuille/sac/passeport.**

M **MAIL** *(courrier).* See also POST OFFICES. If you don't know ahead of time where you'll stay in Paris, you can have mail addressed to you c/o Poste Restante, 52, rue du Louvre, 75001 Paris, which is Paris's main post office open 24 hours a day, every day.

The American Express at 11, rue Scribe, 75009 Paris, also holds mail. Take your passport with you to claim it.

Have you any mail for…?	**Avez-vous du courrier pour…?**

MAPS. Small maps of the city *(plan)* are given away at tourist offices, banks and hotels. More detailed maps are sold in bookshops and at newsstands. A good investment is the compact map book "Plan de Paris" put out by A. Leconte. It contains a large fold-out map and small detailed ones of each *arrondissement,* with useful addresses. Falk-Verlag, Hamburg (the map producer for this book) also publishes a good **116** map of Paris.

MEDICAL CARE. See also EMERGENCIES and HEALTH. To be at ease, make sure your health insurance policy covers any illness or accident while on holiday. If not, ask your insurance representative, automobile association or travel agent for details of special travel insurance.

Visitors from E.E.C. countries with corresponding health insurance facilities are entitled to medical and hospital treatment under the French social security system. Before leaving home, make sure you find out about necessary formalities and forms.

Paris has excellent doctors, surgeons and medical facilities. Most better hotels and the consulates have a list of English-speaking doctors and dentists. Doctors who belong to the French social security system *(médecins conventionnés)* charge the minimum.

Two private hospitals serve the Anglo-American community: American Hospital of Paris, 63, bd Victor-Hugo, 92202 Neuilly, tel. 47.47.53.00; Hôpital Franco-Britannique, 48, rue de Villiers, Levallois-Perret; tel. 47.58.13.12.

Chemists *(pharmacies)* with green crosses are helpful in dealing with minor ailments or in finding a nurse *(infirmière)* if you need injections or other special care. The Pharmacie des Champs-Elysées, 84, av. des Champs-Elysées, tel. 45.62.02.41, is open 24 hours a day.

Where's the chemist on duty?	**Où est la pharmacie de garde?**
I need a doctor/dentist.	**Il me faut un médecin/dentiste.**
I've a pain here.	**J'ai mal ici.**
an upset stomach	**mal à l'estomac**
a fever	**de la fièvre**
headache	**mal à la tête**

MEETING PEOPLE. Cafés are a source of casual encounters and sometimes friendship, especially among the younger crowd in the Latin Quarter. You can also meet French people through a programme called Meet the French, a private organization which proposes personalized guide service (see GUIDES AND INTERPRETERS).

French people always kiss very close friends on both cheeks (sometimes more than once) and shake hands to greet or say goodbye to old and new friends and acquaintances.

Hello.	**Bonjour.**
I'm glad to meet you.	**Enchanté.**
How are you?	**Comment allez-vous?**

METRO. Paris's underground transport is possibly the world's most efficient, fastest and cleanest. It's also cheaper than most. Express lines (R.E.R.) get you into town in about 15 minutes, with a few stops in between.

You should buy a book of tickets *(carnet)*, available for first or second class, if you plan to take the Métro more than a few times.

For longer stays and lots of travel, you can buy an orange identity card *(carte orange)* valid for a week or a month on buses and the Métro. There are also special tourist tickets, called "Paris Sésame", for two, four or seven days, allowing unlimited travel on bus or Métro. For prices, see p. 103.

Big maps in every Métro station make the system easy to use. The service starts at 5.30 a.m. and ends around 1 a.m. See map on p. 128.

R.A.T.P., the Paris Transport Authority, has an information office at 53ter, quai des Grands-Augustins, 75271 Paris, Cedex 6. You can call them at 43.46.14.14, round the clock, for information on public transport in Paris.

Which line should I take for…?	**Quelle direction dois-je prendre pour…?**

N **NEWSPAPERS and MAGAZINES** *(journal; revue).* In addition to the local French dailies, you'll find the Paris-based *International Herald Tribune* almost everywhere and several English newspapers at many news-stands. *Pariscope* is the best known of the weekly information magazines on sale. A wide range of magazines in English and other languages is available at larger news-stands.

P **PHOTOGRAPHY** *(photographie).* Beautiful shots to be taken at so many street corners make Paris a photographer's dream. The city's hazy atmosphere and soft colours still inspire artists and photographers as they did the Impressionist painters.

All popular film makes and sizes are available; rapid development is possible, though sometimes expensive.

I'd like a film for this camera.	**J'aimerais un film pour cet appareil.**
a black-and-white film	**un film noir et blanc**
a film for colour prints	**un film couleurs**
a colour-slide film	**un film pour diapositives**
How long will it take to develop this film?	**Combien de temps faut-il pour développer ce film?**
May I take a picture?	**Puis-je prendre une photo?**

POLICE *(police)*. In Paris you'll normally see the Police municipale wearing blue uniforms. Also known as Gardiens de la Paix, they direct traffic, help tourists with directions, investigate violations and make arrests.

The C.R.S. police *(Compagnies républicaines de Sécurité)* are responsible to the Ministry of the Interior and often appear *en masse* around the French President's Elysée Palace (usually in dark-blue buses) during important political visits or when demonstrations take place.

The elegantly dressed *Garde républicaine*, often on horse-back and accompanied by a very good band, turn out for ceremonies and parades.

In case of need, you can dial 17 in Paris and all over France for police help.

Where's the nearest police station?	**Où est le commissariat de police le plus proche?**

POST OFFICE and TELEGRAMS *(poste; télégramme)*. See also MAIL and TELEPHONE. You can identify post offices by a sign with a stylized blue bird and the words Postes et Télécommunications *(P & T* or *PTT)*. Paris post offices are open from 8 a.m. to 7 p.m. Mondays to Fridays and 8 a.m. to noon on Saturdays. Stamps may also be bought at tobacconists.

In addition to normal mail service, you can make local or long-distance telephone calls, send telegrams and receive or send money through the post office. The Paris Tourist Information Office has a list of post offices open on Sundays and holidays for telephone and telegraph services. You can send telegrams in English by telephoning 42.33.21.11.

Letters may be delivered within hours in the Paris district by sending them *postexpress* from the post office. Another quick and even cheaper system for delivering a message is the *message téléphoné*. Inquire at the post office of your hotel.

A stamp for this letter/postcard, please.	**Un timbre pour cette lettre/carte postale, s'il vous plaît.**
I want to send a telegram to...	**J'aimerais envoyer un télégramme à...**

PUBLIC HOLIDAYS *(jour férié)*. Following are the French national holidays. Remember that traffic is especially heavy on summer vacation dates. Public offices and banks, as well as shops, are closed on holidays, although you may find an occasional bakery or small food shop open.

January 1	*Jour de l'An*	New Year's Day
May 1	*Fête du Travail*	Labour Day
May 8	*Fête de la Libération*	Victory Day (1945)
July 14	*Fête Nationale*	Bastille Day
August 15	*Assomption*	Assumption
November 1	*Toussaint*	All Saints' Day
November 11	*Anniversaire de l'Armistice*	Armistice Day
December 25	*Noël*	Christmas Day
Movable dates:	*Lundi de Pâques*	Easter Monday
	Ascension	Ascension
	Lundi de Pentecôte	Whit Monday

Are you open tomorrow?   **Etes-vous ouvert demain?**

R **RADIO and TV** *(radio; télévision).* There are three main state-run TV channels in France. Some hotels have television in the lounges, many in the top categories have sets in the rooms.

BBC programmes can be heard on short or medium-wave radios. In summer the French radio broadcasts news and information in English.

RELIGIOUS SERVICES *(offices religieux).* France is a predominantly Roman Catholic country. Mass *(la messe)* in English is said at St. Joseph's Roman Catholic Church, 50, av. Hoche; tel. 45.63.20.61.

There are three principal Anglo-American Protestant churches where services *(le culte)* are held in English:

The American Cathedral (Episcopal), 23, av. George-V; tel. 47.20.17.92

The American Church (interdenominational), 65, quai d'Orsay; tel. 47.05.97.99

St. Michael's Anglican Church, 5, rue d'Aguesseau; tel. 47.42.70.88

The main synagogue in Paris is at 44, rue de la Victoire; tel. 45.26.91.89

T **TAXIS** *(taxi).* You can find taxis cruising around or at the many stands all over town. You can also ring for radio-taxis, though they charge meter-fare for the trip to pick you up. For fares, see p. 103. You'll pay according to rates posted on the cab window, not just the price indicated on the meter (for example, extra charges for luggage).

TELEPHONE *(téléphone)*. Long-distance and international calls can be made from any phone box, but if you need assistance in placing the call, go to the post office or get your hotel to do it. (If you make a call from your hotel, a café or a restaurant, you are likely to be charged a little extra.)

There are two types of payphones. One takes a range of coins, the other is card operated. Telecards are sold at post offices, railway ticket counters and shops recognized by a ''Télécarte'' sign, and are available for 40 or 120 charge units.

For long-distance calls within France, there are no area codes (just dial the 8-digit number of the person you want to call), *except* when telephoning from Paris or the Paris region to the provinces (dial 16 and wait for the dialling tone, then dial the 8-digit number of the subscriber) and from the provinces to Paris or the Paris region (dial 16, wait for the dialling tone, then dial 1 followed by the 8-digit number). If you need the assistance of an operator, dial 36.10.

To ring abroad from France, dial 19 followed, after the change of tone, by the country's number (listed in all boxes), the area code and the subscriber's number. If direct dialling is not available to that country or if you don't know the telephone number of the subscriber, dial 19 and wait for the tone, then dial 33 followed by the code number of the country in question to reach the operator (UK 44, U.S.A. and Canada 1). If you do not know the number of the country, call the international information, 19.33.33.

It's cheaper to make long-distance trunk calls after 8 p.m.

TIME DIFFERENCES. France follows Greenwich Mean Time + 1, and in summer the clocks are put forward one hour.

Summer chart:

New York	London	**Paris**	Sydney	Auckland
6 a.m.	11 a.m.	**noon**	8 p.m.	10 p.m.

TIPPING *(pourboire)*. A 10 to 15 per cent service charge is generally included automatically in hotel and restaurant bills. Rounding off the overall bill helps round off friendships with waiters, too. It is also in order to hand the bellboys, doormen, filling station attendants, etc., a coin or two for their service.

T Some suggestions:

Hotel porter, per bag	4–5 F
Hotel maid, per week	20–40 F
Lavatory attendant	2 F
Waiter	5–10% (optional)
Taxi driver	10–15%
Hairdresser/Barber	15% (gen. incl.)
Tour guide	10%

TOILETS (*toilettes*). Paris is improving its public toilets, though sanitary standards are still far from perfect. Those near important Métro stops are generally modern and quite clean. Café W.C.'s are usually free, but you should order at least a coffee if you use the toilet. A saucer with small change on it means a tip is expected. If the toilet has no light-switch, the light will go on when you lock the door. The women's toilets may be marked *Dames*, the men's either *Messieurs* or *Hommes*.

Where are the toilets, please?   **Où sont les toilettes, s'il vous plaît?**

TOURIST INFORMATION OFFICES (*office du tourisme*). Paris's main Tourist Information Office is extremely efficient: 127, Champs-Elysées, 75008 Paris; tel. 47.23.61.72. They offer abundant documentation and a currency-exchange office. Other branches of the tourist office are located in major stations, airports and terminals.

For a selection of the principal weekly events in English, call 47.20.88.98.

For detailed information on Paris and surrounding *départements,* you can also contact the C.R.T.L., Loisirs en Ile-de-France, 19, rue Barbet Jouy, 75007 Paris; tel. 45.51.71.28.

French tourist offices abroad:

Australia   BNP House, 12 Castlereagh Street, Sydney N.S.W. 2000; tel. (612) 231.52.44

Canada   1840 Ouest, rue Sherbrooke, Montreal, Que. H3H 1E4, P.Q.; tel. (514) 931-3855
1 Dundas Street W, Suite 2405, P.O. Box 8, Toronto, Ont. M5G 1Z3; tel. (416) 361-1605

| U.K. | 178, Piccadilly, London W1V 0AL; tel. (01) 493 6594 | **T** |

U.S.A. 645 N. Michigan Avenue, Suite 430, Chicago, IL 60611; tel. (312) 337-6301

9401 Wilshire Boulevard, Room 840, Beverly Hills, CA 90212; tel. (213) 271-6665

610 Fifth Avenue, New York, NY 10020; tel. (212) 757-1125

Post Street, Suite 601, San Francisco, CA 94108; tel. (415) 982-7272

TRAINS *(train)*. The French National Railways *(Société des Chemins de Fer Français* or S.N.C.F.) run fast, punctual and comfortable trains. Excellent high-speed services (TGV—*train à grande vitesse*) operate on selected routes.

The main stations in Paris are Gare du Nord (for British connections), Gare de l'Est, Gare d'Austerlitz, Gare Saint-Lazare and Gare de Lyon (for links with the Riviera, Spain and Italy). Various categories of tickets are available (see p. 101). Make sure to get your ticket punched *before* getting on board, by inserting it in one of the orange machines (called a *machine à composter* or *composteur*) on the way to the platform. If it is not clipped and dated, the conductor *(contrôleur)* is entitled to fine you on the train. Tickets purchased abroad need not be punched.

WATER *(eau)*. Tap water is safe in Paris and all over the country, except when marked *eau non potable* (unsafe for drinking). Several kinds of mineral water are sold everywhere. See also HEALTH.   **W**

a bottle of mineral water	**une bouteille d'eau minérale**
fizzy (carbonated)/still	**gazeuse/non gazeuse**

YOUTH HOSTELS *(auberge de jeunesse)*. For visitors between 16 and 30, a pamphlet "Youth Welcome" lists more than 20 centres, accommodation and prices. Write to the tourist office asking for this list, then reserve in advance at the hostel of your choice.   **Y**

Other useful addresses are:

Fédération Unie des Auberges de Jeunesse, 6, rue Mesnil, 75116 Paris; tel. 42.61.84.03

Centre d'information et de documentation de la jeunesse, 101, quai Branly, 75015 Paris; tel. 45.66.40.20   **123**

SOME USEFUL EXPRESSIONS

yes/no	**oui/non**
please/thank you	**s'il vous plaît/merci**
excuse me	**excusez-moi**
you're welcome	**je vous en prie**
where/when/how	**où/quand/comment**
how long/how far	**combien de temps/à quelle distance**
yesterday/today/tomorrow	**hier/aujourd'hui/demain**
day/week/month/year	**jour/semaine/mois/année**
left/right	**gauche/droite**
up/down	**en haut/en bas**
good/bad	**bon/mauvais**
big/small	**grand/petit**
cheap/expensive	**bon marché/cher**
hot/cold	**chaud/froid**
old/new	**vieux/neuf**
open/closed	**ouvert/fermé**
Where are the toilets?	**Où sont les toilettes?**
Does anyone here speak English?	**Y a-t-il quelqu'un ici qui parle anglais?**
I don't understand.	**Je ne comprends pas.**
Please write it down.	**Veuillez bien me l'écrire.**
What does this mean?	**Que signifie ceci?**
Waiter/Waitress!	**S'il vous plaît!**
Help me, please.	**Aidez-moi, s'il vous plaît.**
Get a doctor—quickly!	**Un médecin, vite!**
What time is it?	**Quelle heure est-il?**
I'd like…	**J'aimerais...**
How much is that?	**C'est combien?**

DAYS OF THE WEEK

Sunday	**dimanche**	Thursday	**jeudi**
Monday	**lundi**	Friday	**vendredi**
Tuesday	**mardi**	Saturday	**samedi**
Wednesday	**mercredi**		

Index

An asterisk (*) next to a page number indicates a map reference. Page numbers in bold face refer to the main entry.

Selection of Paris Hotels and Restaurants

Where do you start? Choosing a hotel or restaurant in a place you're not familiar with can be daunting. To help you find your way amid the bewildering variety, we have made a few selections from the *Red Guide to France 1986* published by Michelin, the recognized authority on gastronomy and accommodation throughout Europe.

Our own Berlitz criteria have been price and position. In the hotel section, for a single room without bath, Higher-priced means above 900 F, Medium-priced 400–900 F, Lower-priced below 400 F. Similarly, for the restaurants, Higher-priced means above 300 F, Medium-priced 200–300 F, Lower-priced below 200 F. Within each price category, hotels and restaurants are grouped alphabetically according to geographical location. Special features, where applicable, plus regular closing days are given. Annual closing dates may be subject to change, so it is best to check in advance.

For hotel bookings, the French Government Tourist Office at 127, Avenue des Champs-Elysées in Paris will help, and there are reservation desks at Roissy-Charles-de-Gaulle and Orly airports. For both hotels and restaurants, advance reservations are advised.

For a wider choice of hotels and restaurants, we strongly recommend you obtain the authoritative Michelin *Red Guide to France*, which gives a comprehensive and reliable picture of the situation throughout the country.

HOTELS

HIGHER-PRICED (above 900 F)

Inter-Continental,
3 rue de Castiglione
75001*
Tel. 42.60.37.80
Tlx. 220114
Rôtisserie Rivoli. Café Tuileries.
Outdoor dining.

Lotti
7 rue de Castiglione
75001
Tel. 42.60.37.34
Tlx. 240066

Ritz
15 place Vendôme
75001
Tel. 42.60.38.30
Tlx. 220262
Ritz-Espadon restaurant. Delight-
ful indoor garden.

Westminster
13 rue de la Paix
75002
Tel. 42.61.57.46
Tlx. 680035
Le Céladon restaurant.

Sofitel Bourbon
32 rue St-Dominique
75007
Tel. 45.55.91.80
Tlx. 250019
All modern comforts. Le Dauphin
restaurant.

Postal or zip code. The final one
or two figures represent the arron-
dissement or district.

Bristol
112 rue du Faubourg-St-Honoré
75008
Tel. 42.66.91.45
Tlx. 280961
Indoor swimming pool. Garden.

Concorde-St-Lazare
108 rue St-Lazare
75008
Tel. 42.94.22.22
Tlx. 650442
Café Terminus.

Crillon
10 place de la Concorde
75008
Tel. 42.65.24.24
Tlx. 290204
L'Obélisque and Les Ambassad-
eurs restaurants. Outdoor dining.

Elysées-Marignan
12 rue de Marignan
75008
Tel. 43.59.58.61
Tlx. 660018

George V
31 av. George-V
75008
Tel. 47.23.54.00
Tlx. 650082
Les Princes restaurant. Outdoor
dining.

Lancaster
7 rue de Berri
75008
Tel. 43.59.90.43
Tlx. 640991
Outdoor dining.

3

Plaza-Athénée
25 av. Montaigne
75008
Tel. 47.23.78.33
Tlx. 650092
Régence et Relais Plaza restaurants.

Prince de Galles
33 av. George-V
75008
Tel. 47.23.55.11
Tlx. 280627
Outdoor dining.

Royal Monceau
37 av. Hoche
75008
Tel. 45.61.98.00
Tlx. 650361
Le Jardin and Le Carpaccio restaurants. Indoor swimming pool. Outdoor dining.

Warwick
5 rue de Berri
75008
Tel. 45.63.14.11
Tlx. 642295
La Couronne restaurant.

Le Grand Hôtel
2 rue Scribe
75009
Tel. 42.68.12.13
Tlx. 220875
Le Patio and Café de la Paix restaurants.

Scribe
1 rue Scribe
75009
Tel. 47.42.03.40,
Tlx. 214653
Le Jardin des Muses restaurant.

Hilton
18 av. de Suffren
75015
Tel. 42.73.92.00
Tlx. 200955
All modern comforts. Le Toit de Paris restaurant with lovely view over Paris. Western and La Terrasse restaurants. Outdoor dining.

Montparnasse Park Hôtel
19 rue Cdt-Mouchotte
75014
Tel. 43.20.15.51
Tlx. 200135
All modern comforts. View. Outdoor dining. Montparnasse 25 and La Ruche restaurants.

Nikko
61 quai de Grenelle
75015
Tel. 45.75.62.62
Tlx. 260012
All modern comforts. View. Indoor swimming pool. Les Célébrités and Brasserie Pont Mirabeau restaurants and Benkay Japanese restaurant.

Baltimore
88 bis av. Kléber
75116
Tel. 45.53.83.33
Tlx. 611591
All modern comforts. L'Estournel restaurant.

La Pérouse
40 rue La Pérouse
75116
Tel. 45.00.83.47
Tlx. 613420
All modern comforts. Restaurant l'Astrolabe.

Concorde Lafayette
3 pl. du Gén-Koenig
75017
Tel. 47.58.12.84
Tlx. 650892
L'Etoile d'Or, L'Arc-en-Ciel restaurants and Les Saisons coffee shop. Panoramic bar on 34th floor.

Méridien
81 bd. Gouvion-St-Cyr
75017
Tel. 47.58.12.30
Tlx. 290952
All modern comforts. Le Clos de Longchamp, Café l'Arlequin, Le Yamato (Japanese) and La Maison Beaujolaise restaurants.

MEDIUM-PRICED (400–900 F)

Duminy Vendôme
3 rue du Mont-Thabor
75001
Tel. 42.60.32.80
Tlx. 213492

France et Choiseul
239 rue St-Honoré
75001
Tel. 42.61.54.60
Tlx. 680959
Outdoor dining.

Louvre-Concorde
pl. A.-Malraux
75001
Tel. 42.61.56.01
Tlx. 220412

Mayfair
3 rue Rouget-de-Lisle
75001
Tel. 42.60.38.14
Tlx. 240037
All modern comforts.

Atlantide
114 bd. Richard-Lenoir
75011
Tel. 43.38.29.29
Tlx. 216907
All modern comforts.

Holiday Inn
10 pl. de la République
75011
Tel. 43.55.44.34
Tlx. 210651
All modern comforts. Belle Epoque restaurant and Le Jardin d'Hiver coffee shop. Outdoor dining.

Lutèce
65 rue St-Louis-en-l'Ile
75004
Tel. 43.26.23.52

Abbaye St-Germain
10 rue Cassette
75006
Tel. 45.44.38.11
All modern comforts. Quiet situation. Garden.

Littré
9 rue Littré
75006
Tel. 45.44.38.68
Tlx. 203852
Quiet situation.

Lutétia
45 bd. Raspail
75006
Tel. 45.44.38.10
Tlx. 270424
*Le Paris restaurant and brasserie
Lutétia.*

Relais Christine
3 rue Christine
75006
Tel. 43.26.71.80
Tlx. 202606
All modern comforts. Quiet situation.

Victoria Palace
6 rue Blaise-Desgoffe
75006
Tel. 45.44.38.16
Tlx. 270557

Cayré-Copatel
4 bd. Raspail
75007
Tel. 45.44.38.88
Tlx. 270577
All modern comforts.

Pont Royal
7 rue de Montalembert
75007
Tel. 45.44.38.27
Tlx. 270113
Les Antiquaires restaurant.

Résidence Elysées Maubourg
35 bd. de La-Tour-Maubourg
75007
Tel. 45.56.10.78
Tlx. 206227
All modern comforts.

6

St-Simon
14 rue de St-Simon
75007
Tel. 45.48.35.66
Attractively furnished.

Château-Frontenac
54 rue P.-Charron
75008
Tel. 47.23.55.85
Tlx. 660994
Pavillon Russe restaurant.

Claridge Bellman
37 rue François-1er
75008
Tel. 47.23.90.03
Tlx. 641150
All modern comforts.

Frantel-Windsor
14 rue Beaujon
75008
Tel. 45.63.04.04
Tlx. 650902
*All modern comforts. Le Clovis
restaurant.*

Napoléon
40 av. de Friedland
75008
Tel. 47.66.02.02
Tlx. 640609
Napoléon Baumann restaurant.

Royal Malesherbes
24 bd. Malesherbes
75008
Tel. 42.65.53.30
Tlx. 660190
All modern comforts.

Brébant
32 bd. Poissonnière
75009
Tel. 47.70.25.55
Tlx. 280127
All modern comforts.

Commodore
12 bd. Haussmann
75009
Tel. 42.46.72.82
Tlx. 280601

**Mercure Paris Porte
de Versailles**
rue Moulin
92170 Vanves
Tel. 46.42.93.22
Tlx. 202195

P.L.M. St-Jacques
17 bd. St-Jacques
75014
Tel. 45.89.89.80
Tlx. 270740
All modern comforts. Café Français and Le Patio restaurants.

Sofitel Paris
8 rue L.-Armand
75015
Tel. 45.54.95.00
Tlx. 200432
All modern comforts. Indoor swimming pool with panoramic view. Le Relais de Sèvres restaurant and La Tonnelle brasserie.

Résidence du Bois
16 rue Chalgrin
75116
Tel. 45.00.50.59
Quiet situation. Attractive furnishings. Garden.

Rond-Point de Longchamp
86 rue de Longchamp
75116
Tel. 45.05.13.63
Tlx. 620653
All modern comforts. Belles Feuilles restaurant.

Union H. Etoile
44 rue Hamelin
75116
Tel. 45.53.14.95
Tlx. 611394
All modern comforts.

Mercure
27 av. des Ternes
75017
Tel. 47.66.49.18
Tlx. 650679
All modern comforts.

Regent's Garden
6 rue P.-Demours
75017
Tel. 45.74.07.30
Tlx. 640127
Quiet situation. Attractive garden.

Splendid Etoile
1 bis av. Carnot
75017
Tel. 47.66.41.41
Tlx. 280773
All modern comforts.

Mercure Paris Montmartre
1 rue Caulaincourt
75018
Tel. 42.94.17.17
Tlx. 640605
All modern comforts.

Mercure Porte de Pantin
25 rue Scandicci
93500 Pantin
Tel. 48.46.70.66
Tlx. 230742
All modern comforts.

Terrass'Hôtel
12 rue J.-de-Maistre
75018
Tel. 46.06.72.85
Tlx. 280830
All modern comforts. Le Guerlande and l'Albaron restaurants.

LOWER-PRICED (below 400 F)

Family
35 rue Cambon
75001
Tel. 42.61.54.84

Montana Tuileries
12 rue St-Roch
75001
Tel. 42.60.35.10
Tlx. 214404
All modern comforts.

Du Piémont
22 rue de Richelieu
75001
Tel. 42.96.44.50

Richepanse
14 rue Richepanse
75001
Tel. 42.60.36.00
Tlx. 210811

Bretonnerie
22 rue Ste-Croix-de-la-Bretonnerie
75004
Tel. 48.87.77.63

Deux Iles
59 rue St.-Louis-en-l'Ile
75004
Tel. 43.26.13.35

Méridional
36 bd. Richard-Lenoir
75011
Tel. 48.05.75.00
Tlx. 211324

Angleterre
44 rue Jacob
75006
Tel. 42.60.34.72

Madison Hôtel
143 bd. St-Germain
75006
Tel. 43.29.72.50
Tlx. 201628

Odéon Hôtel
3 rue de l'Odéon
75006
Tel. 43.25.90.67
Tlx. 206731
All modern comforts.

Scandinavia
27 rue de Tournon
75006
Tel. 43.29.67.20
In beautiful rustic setting.

Bersoly's
28 rue de Lille
75007
Tel. 42.60.73.79

La Bourdonnais
111 av. de La Bourdonnais
75007
Tel. 47.05.45.42
Tlx. 201416
*La Cantine des Gourmets
restaurant.*

Derby Hôtel
5 av. Dusquesne
75007
Tel. 47.05.12.05
Tlx. 206236

Suède
31 rue Vaneau
75007
Tel. 47.05.00.08
Tlx. 200596

Elysées Ponthieu
24 rue de Ponthieu
75008
Tel. 42.25.68.70
Tlx. 640053
All modern comforts.

Lord Byron
5 rue Chateaubriand
75008
Tel. 43.59.89.98
Tlx. 649662
Garden.

Plaza Haussmann
177 bd. Haussmann
75008
Tel. 45.63.93.83
Tlx. 643716
All modern comforts.

Rond-Point des Champs-Elysées
10 rue de Ponthieu
75008
Tel. 43.59.55.58
Tlx. 642386

Blanche Fontaine
34 rue Fontaine
75009
Tel. 45.26.72.32
Tlx. 660311
Quiet situation.

Franklin et du Brésil
19 rue Buffault
75009
Tel. 42.80.27.27
Tlx. 640988
Les Années Folles restaurant.

Paris Est
Cour d'Honneur
75010
Tel. 42.41.00.33
Tlx. 217916
All modern comforts.

Terminus Nord
12 bd. Denain
75010
Tel. 42.80.20.00
Tlx. 660615

Equinoxe
40 rue Le-Brun
75013
Tel. 43.37.56.56
Tlx. 201476
All modern comforts.

Modern Hôtel Lyon
3 rue Parrot
75012
Tel. 43.43.41.52
Tlx. 230369

Paris-Lyon-Palace
11 rue de Lyon
75012
Tel. 43.07.29.49
Tlx. 213310

Relais de Lyon
64 rue Crozatier
75012
Tel. 43.44.22.50
Tlx. 216690
All modern comforts.

L'Aiglon
232 bd. Raspail
75014
Tel. 43.20.82.42

Waldorf
17 rue du Départ
75014
Tel. 43.20.64.79
Tlx. 201677
All modern comforts.

Wallace
89 rue Fondary
Tel. 45 78 83 30
Tlx. 205277
All modern comforts.

Fremiet
6 av. Fremiet
75016
Tel. 45.24.52.06
Tlx. 630329
Quiet situation.

Massenet
5 bis rue Massenet
75116
Tel. 45.24.43.03
Tlx. 620682

Régina de Passy
6 rue de la Tour
75116
Tel. 45.24.43.64
Tlx. 630004

Magellan
17 rue J.-B.-Dumas
75017,
Tel. 45.72.44.51
Tlx. 660728
Quiet situation.

Capucines Montmartre
5 rue A.-Bruant
75018
Tel. 42.52.89.80

Regyn's Montmartre
18 place des Abbesses
75018
Tel. 42.54.45.21

Airport

Hilton Orly
94396 Val-de-Marne
Tel. 46.87.33.88
Tlx. 250621
All modern comforts. Near airport railway station. View. Le Café du Marché and La Louisiane restaurants.

Holiday Inn
1 allée Verger
95500 Roissy-en-France
Tel. 49.88.00.22
Tlx. 695143
All modern comforts.

RESTAURANTS

HIGHER-PRICED (above 300 F)

Ritz-Espadon
15 place Vendôme
75001
Tel. 42.60.38.30
Outdoor dining.

Grand Vefour
17 rue de Beaujolais
75001
Tel. 42.96.56.27
Late 18th-century. Closed Saturday and Sunday.

Tour d'Argent (Terrail)
15 quai de Tournelle
75005
Tel. 43.54.23.31
Lovely view of Notre-Dame. In the cellars, a historical exhibit on wine. Closed Monday.

Les Ambassadeurs
10 place de la Concorde
75008
Tel. 42.65.24.24
18th-century setting. Outdoor dining.

Bristol
112 rue du Faubourg-St-Honoré
75008
Tel. 42.66.91.45

Lasserre
17 av. Franklin-D.-Roosevelt
75008
Tel. 43.59.53.43
Closed Sunday and Monday.

Laurent
41 av. Gabriel
75008
Tel. 47.23.79.18
Closed Saturday lunchtime, Sunday and public holidays.

Lucas-Carton (Senderens)
9 place de la Madeleine
75008
Tel. 42.65.22.90
Authentic early 1900s decor. Closed Saturday and Sunday.

Pavillon Elysée (Lenôtre)
10 av. des Champs-Elysées (1st floor)
75008
Tel. 42.65.85.10
Closed Saturday, Sunday and public holidays.

Régence
25 av. Montaigne
75008
Tel. 47.23.78.33
Outdoor dining.

Les Célébrités
61 quai de Grenelle
75015
Tel. 45.75.62.62
View.

Olympne
8 rue Nicolas-Charlet
75015
Tel. 47.34.86.08
Closed Mounday.

MEDIUM-PRICED (200–300 F)

Le Céladon
13 rue de la Paix
75002
Tel. 42.61.57.46
Closed Saturday and Sunday.

Carré des Feuillants
(Dutournier)
14 rue fr Castiglione
75001
Tel. 42.86.82.82
Closed Saturday and Sunday.

Gérard Besson
5 rue du Coq-Héron
75001
Tel. 42.33.14.74
*Closed Saturday, Sunday and
public holidays.*

Mercure Galant
15 rue des Petits-Champs
75001
Tel. 42.96.98.89
*Closed Saturday lunchtime, Sun-
day and public holidays.*

Quai des Ormes (4e) (Masraff)
72 quai de l'Hôtel de Ville
75004
Tel. 42.74.72.22
Closed Saturday and Sunday.

Benoît
20 rue St-Martin
75004
Tel. 42.72.25.76
Closed Saturday and Sunday.

Ambroisie (Pacaud)
65 quai de la Tournelle
75005
Tel. 46.33.18.65
Closed Sunday and Monday.

Duquesnoy
30 rue des Bernardins
75005
Tel. 43.54.21.13
Closed Saturday and Sunday.

Le Paris
45 bd. Raspail
75006
Tel. 45.44.38.10
Closed Sunday and Monday.

Relais Louis XIII
1 rue du Pont-de-Lodi
75006
Tel. 43.26.75.96
*16th-century setting, with beauti-
ful furnishings. Closed Monday
lunchtime and Sunday.*

Villars Palace
8 rue Descartes
75005
Tel. 43.26.39.08
Closed Saturday lunchtime.

L'Argonne
84 rue de Varenne
75007
Tel. 45.51.47.33
*Closed Saturday lunchtime and
Sunday.*

Le Divellec
107 rue de l'Université
75007
Tel. 45.51.91.96
Closed Sunday and Monday.

12

La Flamberge (Albistur)
12 av. Rapp
75007
Tel. 47.05.91.37
*Closed Saturday lunchtime and
Sunday.*

Jules Verne
2nd floor Eiffel Tower
Tel. 45.55.61.44
Tlx. 205789
View over Paris.

Chiberta
3 rue Arsène-Houssaye
75008
Tel. 45.63.77.90
*Closed Saturday, Sunday and
public holidays.*

Fouquet's Elysées
99 av. des Champs-Elysées (1st
floor)
75008
Tel. 47.23.70.60
Tlx. 648227
Closed Saturday and Sunday.

Lamazère
23 rue de Ponthieu
75008
Tel. 43.59.66.66
Closed Sunday.

Ledoyen
Carre Champs-Elysees
75008
Tel. 42.66.54.77
Closed Sunday.

La Marée
1 rue Daru
75008
Tel. 47.63.52.42
Closed Saturday and Sunday.

Taillevent
15 rue Lamennais
75008
Tel. 45.61.12.90
*Closed Saturday, Sunday and
public holidays.*

Café de la Paix
Place de l'Opéra
75009
Tel. 47.42.97.02

Aquitaine (Mme. Massia)
54 rue de Dantzig
75015
Tel. 48.28.67.38
*Closed Sunday and Monday. Out-
door dining.*

Morot Gaudry
6 rue de la Cavalerie (8th floor)
75015
Tel. 45.67.06.85
*View. Open-air terrace dining.
Closed Saturday and Sunday.*

Relais de Sèvres
8 rue L.-Armand
75015
Tel. 45.54.95.00
Closed Saturday and Sunday.

Faugeron
52 rue de Longchamp
75116
Tel. 47.04.24.53
*Closed Saturday, Sunday and
public holidays.*

Michel Pasquet
59 rue LaFontaine
75016
Tel. 42.88.50.01
*Saturday except 1 Sept.–30 Apr.
and Sunday.*

Toit de Passy (Jacquot)
94 av. P.-Doumer
75016
Tel. 45.24.55.37
*Closed Saturday from 23
Aug.–20 Dec., Sunday and public
holidays.*

Vivarois (Peyrot)
192 av. V.-Hugo
75116
Tel. 45.04.04.31
Closed Saturday and Sunday.

Apicius (Vigato)
122 av. Villiers
75017
Tel. 43.80.19.66
Closed Saturday and Sunday.

Le Bernardin (Le Coze)
18 rue Troyon
75017
Tel. 43.80.40.61
Seafood specialities. Closed Sunday and Monday.

Etoile d'Or
3 place du Gén.-Koenig
75017
Tel. 47.58.12.84
Tlx. 650905

Manoir de Paris
6 rue Pierre-Demours
75017
Tel. 45.72.25.25
Closed Saturday and Sunday

Michel Rostang
20 rue Rennequin
75017
Tel. 47.63.40.77
Tlx. 649629
*Closed Saturday (except evenings
October to March), Sunday and
public holidays.*

Beauvilliers (Carlier)
52 rue Lamarck
75018
Tel. 42.54.54.42
*Unusual decor. Terrace with outdoor dining. Closed Monday
lunchtime and Sunday.*

LOWER-PRICED (below 200 F)

Aux Petits Pères
(Chez Yvonne)
8 rue N.-D.-des-Victoires
75002
Tel. 42.60.91.73
Closed Saturday and Sunday.

Chez Pauline (Génin)
5 rue Villedo
75001
Tel. 42.96.20.70
Closed Saturday evening and Sunday.

Pierre Traiteur
10 rue de Richelieu
75001
Tel. 42.96.09.17
Closed Saturday and Sunday.

Le Péché Mignon (Rousseau)
5 rue Guillaume-Bertrand
75011
Tel. 43.57.02.51
Closed Sunday and Monday.

Jacques Cagna
14 rue des Grands-Augustins
75006
Tel. 43.26.49.39
In old Parisian house. Closed Saturday and Sunday.

Bistrot de Paris
33 rue de Lille
75007
Tel. 42.61.16.83
1900s-style bistro. Closed Saturday lunchtime, Sunday and public holidays.

La Boule d'Or
13 bd de La-Tour-Maubourg
75007
Tel. 47.05.50.18
Closed Saturday lunchtime and Monday.

La Cantine des Gourmets
113 av. de La Bourdonnais
75007
Tel. 47.05.47.96
Closed Sunday and Monday.

Chez les Anges
54 bd de La-Tour-Maubourg
75007
Tel. 47.05.89.86
Closed Sunday evening, Monday.

Gildo (Bellini)
153 rue Grenelle
75007
Tel. 45.51.54.12
Italian. Closed Sunday, Monday.

Labrousse
4 rue Pierre-Leroux
75007
Tel. 43.06.99.39
Closed Sunday and Monday lunchtime.

Pantagruel (Israël)
20 rue de l'Exposition
75007
Tel. 45.51.79.96
Closed Saturday lunchtime and Sunday.

Récamier (Cantegrit)
4 rue Récamier
75007
Tel. 45.48.86.58
Closed Sunday.

Tan Dinh
60 rue Verneuil
75007
Tel. 45.44.04.84
Vietnamese. Closed Sunday.

Copenhague
142 av. des Champs-Elysées
75008
Outdoor dining. Closed Sunday and public holidays.

Les Jardins Lenôtre
(ground floor)
10 av. des Champs-Elysées
75008
Tel. 42.65.85.10

Au Chateaubriant
23 rue Chabrol
75010
Tel. 48.24.58.94
Italian. Collection of paintings. Closed Sunday and Monday.

Chez Michel (Tounissoux)
10 rue de Belzunce
75010
Tel. 48.78.44.14
Closed Friday and Saturday.

Nicolas
12 rue de la Fidélité
75010
Tel. 42.46.84.74
Closed Saturday lunchtime.

Bistro 121
121 rue de Convention
75015
Tel. 45.57.52.90
Closed Sunday evening and Monday.

Pierre Vedel
19 rue Duranton
75015
Tel. 45.58.43.17
Closed Saturday and Sunday.

Guy Savoy
28 rue Duret
75116
Tel. 45.00.17.67
Closed Saturday and Sunday.

Le Petit Bedon (Ignace)
38 rue Pergolèse
75116
Tel. 45.00.23.66
Closed Saturday and Sunday.

Chez Augusta
98 rue de Tocqueville
75017
Tel. 47.63.39.97
Closed Sunday and public holidays.

Michel Comby
116 bd Périere
75017
Tel. 43.80.88.68
Closed Saturday and Sunday.

Le Petit Colombier (Fournier)
42 rue des Acacias
75017
Tel. 43.80.28.54
Closed Sunday lunchtime and Saturday.

Sormani
4 rue du Gén.-Lanrezac
75017
Tel. 43.80.13.91
Italian specialities. Closed Saturday, Sunday and public holidays.

Timgad (Laasri)
21 rue Brunel
75017
Tel. 45.74.23.70
North African specialities. Moorish decor.

Charlot 1er "Merveilles des Mers"
128 bis bd. de Clichy
75018
Tel. 45.22.47.08

Cochon d'Or
192 av. Jean-Jaurès
75019
Tel. 46.07.23.13

Relais Pyrénées (Marty)
1 rue du Jourdain
75020
Tel. 46.36.65.81
Closed Saturday.